WHo tOLD YOU THat?

The truth aBoUt tHe Lies

Gail E. Dudley

Who Told You That?
by Gail E. Dudley
Highly Recommended International, Inc.

Printed in the United States of America

ISBN 978-0-9752921-1-2

Published by Gail E. Dudley
Highly Recommended International, Inc.
Ministry In Motion Ministries International Columbus, Ohio, United States of America
614-441-8178

Cover Design

Shelbi T. Harris
Shel 10, LLC
www.Shel10.com

Editing

Revised Edition – October 2011 Release: Darla Hightower
DH Editorial Services
darlahightower@comcast.net
719-238-1146

May 18, 2011 Release: Stephanie Bright-Mayberry
Bright Ideas Creative Design and Consulting
brightideascreative1@gmail.com

Interior Page Formatting

Kathy Curtis
klcur321@bellsouth.net
www.christianbookformat.com

Beloved,

My prayer is that this book will set you free in the name of Jesus! I pray that you will ask the question, "Who Told You That?" as you read through each chapter. I want that question to be so imbedded in your spirit that you will be reminded to search for the truth according to God, and that you will remember you are made in the image of God. It's good. It's very good!

The chapters you will read are not long. However, I ask that you take your time in reading. Let the words penetrate your heart. Reflect, remember, digest, let the words cut deep, but then, release, and be set free in the name of Jesus. Let's get started! Take a moment and consider the things that have been told to you or about you. Now ask yourself: Who Told You That?

ACKNOWLEDGMENTS

This work is God's favor upon me who continues to speak truth into my spirit. I was once lost, but He saved me from the lies of the enemy.

This book is dedicated to my daughter,
Dominiq Rae Dudley, on her seventeenth birthday.

This book is possible because of the greatest husband in the world, Reverend Dr. Kevin R. Dudley. You rock! I am honored to have such an anointed man who supports me and loves me 100 percent.

Special thanks to my son, Alexander, for simply keeping it real.

Thank you, Shelbi, of Shel 10, llc, for the outstanding cover design.

Finally, I am indebted to each editor; Stephanie Bright-Mayberry, for meeting the deadlines in order to have this book released on my daughter's birthday. Mary Owens for helping me set the book up for its revised edition in order to hand it off to a former editor of NavPress, Darla Hightower, who is the owner of DH Editorial Services, and Kathy Curtis for the interior page formatting.

Contents

FOREWORD

"Who told you that?" is a question that we all should ask when information is passed along to us, when statements are made about others or situations, and in our everyday conversations.

I once received an email that was accusing a company of wrongdoing. Before the email reached me, it had been forwarded to many other people. After reading the accusation, I sent an email back to the woman who had sent it to me and asked "Who told you that?" Imagine the woman's embarrassment when after researching the accusation, the person found it to be false. This woman had to send out an apology to everyone she forwarded the email to.

Just because something is said does not necessarily mean that it is the truth. We must ask the question "Who told you that?" to ensure we are getting accurate information.

Oftentimes when we receive information, it is very easy to be misguided, especially with regard to the

Christian faith. I know for myself, growing up in the Baptist church, I was misguided by traditions disguised as God's "commandments." I'm not sure how it got started, but I would speculate and say that it was handed down from generation to generation.

One of the many things I was taught to believe was that it was wrong for a woman to wear pants to church. I actually believed for many years that a woman could go to hell for wearing pants in the church. Where does it say that in the Word of God?

I have to wonder how many people have been kept out of the church or who chose not to be a part of a church body because of traditions that do not line up with the Word of God. Where does it say in the Word of God that if you are a Pastor's wife, you must utilize the title "First Lady" and sit on the first or second row? Again, who told you that? Who said that a woman's hemline had to be below her knee? Who said that you have to dress in your "Sunday best" to come to church? Who told you that? The list goes on and on.

Gail is one who firmly believes and lives by the Word of God. She embraces the truth. If it doesn't line up with the Word, the first thing that will come out of her mouth is "Who told you that?"

Who Told You That? was birthed from a series of conferences that Gail has shared through the nation. Gail's approach is direct as she delivers the truth according to the Word of God. She cuts to the chase and does not sugarcoat anything. She is not afraid to stand for what is right, even if that means standing alone. Gail is in ministry to equip the body of Christ with the necessary tools in order for the body to have an abundant life in Jesus Christ.

Who Told You That? will expose the lies of the enemy and cause you to examine your own conversations, traditions, and beliefs. *Who Told You That?* will cause you to take action and begin to ask the right questions of yourself and others. "Who told you that?"

Kelly L. Shaw
Preparing For God's Choosing
"Spiritual Boot Camp"
kelkeepinitreal@yahoo.com

VERY GOOD

Please allow me to cut through everything and get to the point of this book and work backward.

Genesis 1:1 says, "In the beginning God created the heavens and the earth." Over and over again throughout the first chapter of Genesis, God says, "Let us" and then He saw that "it was good." When we arrive at Genesis 1:27, we read, "So God created man in his own image, in the image of God he created him; male and female he created them." *Hold on. I'm about to get to the point.* As we continue to read this chapter, we read these words again in the last verse of this chapter, "God saw all that he had made, and it was very good."

It's all good. So, what's up with the woman in Genesis 3? What in the world happened? She, like many of us today, allowed others to whisper into her ears lies that filled her mind with false information. You already know the story that I will recap in my personal paraphrase. God said it was not good for man to be alone so He caused man to sleep and from man came woman. Yep, good. It was so good that Genesis 2:24 says, "For this reason a man will leave his father and mother and be united to his wife, and they will become one flesh."

Then here comes the serpent, a slick, crafty, deceitful, and clever being. He trips the woman up by asking her, "Did God really say...?" After she opens her mouth to respond, he returns with these words, "For God knows that when you eat of it your eyes will be opened, and you will be like God." Back up! Genesis 1:27 says, "So God created man in his own image, the image of God." This means that she was already like God. This is where we get things twisted. We allow others to speak something into our lives to confuse us, even when we already know the truth. Come on. Let us study to show ourselves approved. It is important to know the Word so we don't get tripped up. You see, this is our challenge. We say we love God. We say we worship, adore, and praise Him. But do we really know Him and know His Word?

There are many methods to studying the Bible, however, I would like to call your attention to the "Inductive Study Method." This method draws you into personal interaction with the Scriptures. Inductive Bible study consists of three components:

- Observation—"What does the passage of scripture say?" This is the foundation that must be laid first if you want to accurately interpret and have right application for God's Word. It's discovering what is being said—and this requires time and practice.

Taking time to observe scriptures leads to correct interpretation and provides the foundation for personal application.

- Interpretation—"What does this passage of scripture mean?" The basis for accurate interpretation is always careful observation. This is the process of discovering what the passage of scripture means. As you observe Scripture, the meaning will become apparent. One effective way to discover the meaning of a passage is by examining key words and consulting related cross-references.

- Application —answers the question "How does the meaning of this passage of scripture apply to me?" This is usually the first thing we want to know. Application takes place as you are confronted with the truth and decide to respond in obedience to that truth.

As you use this method of study, you will discover God's truth yourself, without leaning on the opinions and commentary of others. This method can be your personal discovery, which develops your confidence in understanding God's message of love personally to you. In the back of this book under the section called, "DARE" you will have an opportunity to review the complete inductive study method.

Theologians would say, "Let us exegesis the text." But in the words of Gail Dudley, "Let us break down the text." The Bible says in 2 Timothy 2:15 (KJV) that we should *"Study to show thyself approved unto God, a work-man that needeth not to be ashamed, rightly dividing the word of truth."* If we would study the Bible, we would be better prepared to respond if and when a response is needed. If we would spend time with God, we would know when someone is trying to deceive us and distract us from focusing on what is true. If we would walk in the confidence of the Lord, we would be free from shame. If we would study His Word, we would be able to rightly divide the word of truth. We would be able to say, as Nehemiah said to the messenger sent to distract him, *"There is no truth in any part of your story. You are making up the whole thing."* (Nehemiah 6:8, NLT) More on this in the next chapter, but for now, as we look back at Genesis 3, the woman fell into the serpent's trap. The question is, Why?

Basically, the serpent was telling the woman that she was "less than." He was telling her that she was not made in the image of God.

Today, we will allow people to tell us that we are not created in the image of God. We will believe the lie that we are not "good enough." We will respond to the lie by trying to prove that we are "good enough," allowing others to know that they have rattled our foundation. Once we let people know that they have shaken us, watch out. They will continue to feed us filth, and if we are not careful, we will find ourselves with our minds spinning out of control.

Psalms 139 says, *We are "fearfully and wonderfully made."* If that's true, and God says that it is, then why do we walk around hopelessly confused about who we are? Why do we allow the enemy's lies to take hold of us?

The woman in Genesis 1 believed the hype and ate of the tree of the knowledge of good and evil, even though God had said not to eat from it. So many of us get caught up in what is not true that we will read the Bible through the lens of another and misinterpret the Word of God. We will believe the lies told to us from others and pretend to be someone we are not. We will go on crash diets, wear clothes not made for us, purchase items we cannot afford, are in relationships that are clearly toxic and unequally yoked, act certain ways in certain places because of how we think we are supposed to act, believe what is told to us about the Bible even when it doesn't sound quite right, and the list goes on and on.

Isn't it interesting that after the serpent was temporarily successful with his deceit with the woman, he disappeared? Let's look back at the scripture. In Genesis 3:8-10, we find that in the cool of the day when God appeared, both the man and the woman hid after sewing leaves together to make clothing. When God asked, "Where are you?" the man replied, "I heard you walking in the garden, and I was afraid because I was naked; so I hid." And God said, "Who told you that?"

God's question to the man and the woman stirs my spirit. As I become more mature in Christ and in exercising wisdom from the Lord, I find myself asking when faced with issues, dealing with others, and as struggles arise, "Who told you that?" Once the question has been asked, it puts a new light on the things that are being spoken. We must remember that the enemy comes to steal, kill, and destroy, but Jesus comes to bring life in abundance (John 10:10).

Let me be transparent. There have been times that I have fallen for the enemy's tricks. Not everything or everyone deserves a response. In order to prevent falling into the trap of deception, I have had to learn how to guard my conversations. I used to respond quickly and use words to cut people like a knife. It didn't get me anywhere except twisted and tangled into traps that left me wondering how I got myself caught again in dramas wrought with deception.

There are other times that I would sit and listen to people in my life, teachers, friends, previous boyfriends, coworkers, and even family members who would speak negative things into my life that I would take hold of and believe. I would start to believe these things even when I didn't agree. I remember babysitting for a woman who told me that I shouldn't consider going to college because she didn't think I was "college material." So I graduated from high school and cancelled my enrollment to Ohio University because doubt had set in. I began working, purchased my first car, and soon became pregnant. My thoughts were that "this was now my life." That is not what the Lord had for me. Yes, it eventually worked out for my good, but the process was longer and more difficult. This woman, with fuel added to the fire, continued to spew negative things about me, sharing with others in my community that she knew I wouldn't go to college and make anything of myself. Really. She was the one who said that I wasn't college material and planted the seeds of doubt in my head. Had it not been for her comments to me, who knows how those years might have been for me. This is only one of the lies I allowed the enemy to whisper into my spirit. There were others and I will share some of them throughout this book. We all have had things spoken to or about us that have had the ability to take root and create havoc in our lives.

I am truly grateful to have a wonderful husband, a well-educated theologian with dual doctorates, who exposes the truth about the lies we hear so often in church settings. Our church, The Church at North Pointe, in Columbus, Ohio, is a church that experiences "real life" and is intentional in speaking the truth of our Lord and Savior, Jesus Christ. We expose the embedded lies that many have been taught in different churches and break "traditions" formed by man, focusing on the Word of God and making His Word real. I think back to the day that I was told I could not stand with my son in church when he was dedicated to God because I was a single, unwed mother. I remember the guilt and shame I felt because I was unworthy to even hold him while he was being given back to God, because in the church's eyes, I was unworthy. I think about the time I walked into a church in pants and was told I would go to hell for not wearing a dress or skirt. I remember when I was told "God is not pleased with you" because my head was not covered in the church. I can recall so many situations where I believed this nonsense and believed that I always fell short and could not be perfect.

Now I am free from those lies that were told to me. I now know the truth, and I long for you to know the truth about what God sees in you as well.

I am not alone. That is why the Lord has allowed me to release this book in this season. It is time we learn the truth and expose the lies.

My prayer is that this book will set you free from the lies of the enemy. I declare and decree you are delivered and set free in the name of Jesus!

Throughout this book, as lies, thoughts, or your past reveals itself, ask the question, "Who Told You That?" Again, I want this question to be in the forefront of your mind and in your spirit. Please remember that you are fearfully and wonderfully made in the image of Jesus Christ. It's good — it's very good!

We're already on this journey, so let's move forward. Shall we pause a moment and think about all the things that have been told to you, or said about you? Now ask, "Who told you that?"

FaLSE

It's Made Up

Nehemiah was a man who knew the truth and could not be shaken. No matter who tried to deter him from doing what he knew was right and true, he stayed true to what God had called him to do and to say. He responded to Sanballat and his messengers with the same message regardless of how they tried to deceive him.

Let's travel through the beginning of Nehemiah 6:1-4.

> [1] When word came to Sanballat, Tobiah, Geshem the Arab and the rest of our enemies that I had rebuilt the wall and not a gap was left in it — though up to that time I had not set the doors in the gates — [2] Sanballat and Geshem sent me this message: "Come, let us meet together in one of the villages on the plain of Ono."
>
> But they were scheming to harm me; [3] so I sent messengers to them with this reply: "I am carrying on a great project and cannot go down. Why should the work stop while I leave it and go down to you?" [4] Four times

*they sent me the same message, and each time I gave
them the same answer.*

We read in verse 4 that Nehemiah said, "Four times
they sent me the same message, and each time I gave
them the same answer." He would not waver. No one
could get him off course.

How often do people create chaos out of nothing? How
often do people create gossip and cause more damage
than not? Don't believe me? How many times has someone started their conversation with "I heard..."? Let's
give some examples:

> *"I heard that you were involved with..."*
> *"I heard that you were taking his position at your
> company and he was fired because of..."*
> *"I heard you were quitting your job..."*
> *"Are you sure that you should be purchasing that
> home?"*
> *"I hear your company might be downsizing..."*
> *"I saw your son the other day. Shouldn't he be in
> school?"*
> *"I heard you and your ex are getting back together. I
> heard he was with another girl last week..."*
> *"I heard that she..."*

The truth of the matter is that people create gossip in
order to boost their own egos, or to ensure that someone
else doesn't reach a higher "status," or just because they

don't have anything else to talk about. As Nehemiah did not get caught in the trappings of Sanballat's words, we need to stay on course and not get caught in conversations that are unnecessary, unhealthy, and unChristlike. When these conversations find you, learn to be like Nehemiah and stop the "messiness" in its tracks by speaking truth and only truth.

In reading further on through the chapter, the lie was stated as "and not a gap was left in it." Was that really so? When I continue to read Nehemiah 6:1, Nehemiah had not set the doors in the gate. Imagine that. See how messy this can get. The door isn't there yet, therefore, there has to be some sort of gap. Sanballat and his people want to meet with Nehemiah. We should learn to ask the question "Why?" Because of Nehemiah's spirit of discernment and because he knew the Lord, he was able to discern that Sanballat was scheming and that there was a plan to kill him.

I get excited when I read verse 8. "Nothing like what you are saying is happening; you are just making it up out of your head." Although Sanballat sent his aide with an unsealed letter full of lies, hearsay, and twisted truths, Nehemiah did not get off course. His message back was consistent and he did not add nor subtract from it. He was able to guard what he said and his words could not be twisted.

Going back to Genesis 3, the woman responded to the serpent after the serpent asked what God really said. She said, "Of course we may eat fruit from the trees in the garden." It's at this point she should have guarded her conversation. Instead, she continued talking, saying, "It's only the fruit from the tree in the middle of the garden that we are not allowed to eat. God said, 'You must not eat it or even touch it; if you do, you will die.'" Way too much conversation! The enemy only needs an extra bit of information to confuse you and deceive you. Satan is the prince of the power of the air (Ephesians 2:2). And spoken words can fall into the trap of his domain.

The woman's initial reply was enough. However, she continued to talk. After she kept talking, the serpent replied, "Surely you won't die." In today's terminology, we may hear from people around us things like: "Surely you won't get caught," or "Surely you won't get pregnant," or "Surely no one will find out," or "Surely God will still bless you even if you do." Surely you won't . . . you can fill in the blank. There are so many ways to be deceived. "Surely" does not have a face, but "surely" can mess up your life!

Recently, on a flight from San Francisco to Chicago, the plane ran into some turbulence. It was an interesting flight. We began our descent and the plane was about to touch ground when it turned quickly to the left and increased speed, ascending back into the sky. Everyone in the cabin looked around and asked "What's going on?" We could see the ground clearly. The flight attendants advised us that our plane had to quickly ascend due to another plane taking off on the runway where our plane had been cleared to land. That was a close call! The pilot made a large circle to get back into position in order to attempt landing once more. The pilots found themselves back into the position of landing, but once again we returned to ascending, this time because he misjudged his landing. Only at the third attempt did the pilots land the plane without any challenges. This situation challenged my faith. As you know, while flying on a commercial airline you are only able to look out the windows to your left and to your right. You are unable to look out the windows up front. Only the pilot has this opportunity.

Although they are able to see out of the front window, they still rely on the individuals in the towers to give clearance to take off and land. During this flight the people in the tower gave the wrong information twice. I'm glad to know my pilot had the necessary training to make the best decision to return to a higher altitude quickly. Let's face it; sometimes planes crash. Hopefully, the pilot has enough training to know what to do when the situation becomes hairy. Hopefully, each pilot is able to act quickly based on the training they have received, along with their skills to make a quick judgment. As Christians, we must rely upon the discernment of the Lord and upon the leading of the Holy Spirit.

Anything could have happened that day while on that particular flight. To be honest, I was scared. There was a brief moment when I thought this situation could end tragically.

Prior to taking the flight, God had given me an assignment to complete once I returned home, but while on the flight there was a moment I had forgotten what the Lord has spoken to me personally. Bottom line: I didn't believe God that He had more for me. What is up with that? How quickly we allow our flesh to take over our thoughts. I had said "Yes, Lord" earlier but found myself doubting and giving in to Satan when I thought my life was about to end. The enemy is always testing us to see if we will rely on our flesh, his lies, or the truth of the Holy Spirit. It is imperative that we trust God with all our hearts and not lean to our own understanding or the enemy's lies. Due to our assumptions, we can cause a "crash" in our lives and in others. To stop ourselves from listening to and believing the lies of the enemy, may I encourage you to take time to seek Christ and pray. In the name of Jesus, I declare and decree that we stand believing in the Lord as Nehemiah believed and stood with the truth of the Lord saying, "Nothing you are saying is true!" Instead of reacting to our natural thoughts and the lies of the enemy, we must read the Word and wait to hear from God, allowing Him to order and reorder our steps.

Realizing that the enemy uses his well-designed plan to destroy us and move us away from God's plan for us, take a moment to think of what you need in order to fall into Satan's traps.

Looking further in Nehemiah 6, we read:

> [5] *Then, the fifth time, Sanballat sent his aide to me with the same message, and in his hand was an unsealed letter* [6] *in which was written:*

"It is reported among the nations — and Geshem says it is true — that you and the Jews are plotting to revolt, and therefore you are building the wall. Moreover, according to these reports you are about to become their king ⁷and have even appointed prophets to make this proclamation about you in Jerusalem: 'There is a king in Judah!' Now this report will get back to the king; so come, let us confer together."

⁸I sent him this reply: "Nothing like what you are saying is happening; you are just making it up out of your head."

⁹They were all trying to frighten us, thinking, "Their hands will get too weak for the work, and it will not be completed."

But I prayed, "Now strengthen my hands."

Notice what Nehemiah did. He prayed. He didn't speak to anyone but God; he prayed for God to strengthen his hands so he could stay on task. He did not waver.

People of God, when we are faced with making a decision to believe the lie or to believe the truth of the Lord, we must pray. "Now renew my mind and transform my thinking" or "Lord, may I only receive Your truth."

Joyce Meyer states in her book *Battlefield of the Mind* that "through careful strategy and cunning deceit, Satan attempts to set up 'strongholds' in our mind." She goes on to say that "a stronghold is an area in which we are held in bondage (in prison) due to a certain way of thinking." Take a few moments and consider your strongholds—these thought patterns, prison cells, that are your places of bondage. When you think of a prison cell, you don't think of a pretty place. They are dirty, smelly, and small; many are without windows, you sleep on metal beds, paint may be chipping, you are locked behind bars, the toilet without a door for all who pass by to see and hear as you defecate. Prisons and jail cells are not meant for your comfort.

Consider what you must do to release your mind from the emotional and mental state that you may find yourself in at times.

Here are a few questions to consider:

- Do you want to live in this state? Or do you want to be free? If you want to be free from it, what do you need to break down these strongholds?
- "Do not conform any longer to the pattern of this world, but be transformed by the renewing of your mind. Then you will be able to test and approve what God's will is—his good, pleasing and perfect will" (Romans 12:2). What thoughts come to mind? How do you transform and renew your mind?
- "Then you will know the truth, and the truth will set you free" (John 8:32). Are you free or are you focusing on the strongholds set in your mind? Do you know the truth or do you still believe some of the lies that you have been told?

- How can you regain the territory the enemy has stolen from you? (Galatians 6:9) How can you believe the truth of God instead of the lies of the enemy?

Many people are dealing with the enemy within.

"For if you live according to the sinful nature [flesh], you will die; but if by the Spirit you put to death the misdeeds of the body, you will live" (Romans 8:13).

We are called to trust in the Lord with all of our heart, mind, and strength and to allow the Lord, our God, to reveal those things that are not of Him. We are to avail ourselves for His pruning, the cutting or decreasing, of our flesh. Our strength is the strength of the Lord, for we have the Spirit of the Lord living within us. God has given us His Word, the Holy Bible, as a blueprint. However, to the flesh's delight, most Christians are ignorant of the power and access the Lord has handed to each of us. God has given us the keys to the kingdom, but for many of us, we underutilize our keys, and for others, they have thrown the keys away. Some of us are so consumed with the lies of the enemy, we are buried under our own created rubble and cannot fight with the Lord's strength. God called us to "Take up our position" and He also reminded us that we would not have to fight (2 Chronicles). God fights our battles for us. When we fight in our own strength, we will die. Not a physical death, but a spiritual death. We have been called by God to live.

Satan targets our minds. If deceit takes root, it shows in our thoughts, our emotions, and our will. If our minds give in to the enemy, it's over. To protect ourselves against the mind's deceit, we have to fix our mind against the sinfulness of sin and the grace of God. Here's our dilemma: The flesh opposes the heart's desire to do God's will with all its strength. Therefore, we must rely solely on Christ to prevent being tricked. We must keep our minds on the things of Christ as the only way to resist Satan's traps.

Here is a word of caution: reading your Bible and praying just as a habit will not help you. You must give of yourself totally to Christ and be prepared to build a deep and intimate love relationship with Him. Stating that you have read a scripture in the morning is not actually living that scripture that you read. Stating that the Lord is your Shepherd does not necessarily mean that you know the Shepherd. Saying, "now I lay me down to sleep" does not guarantee a restful sleep. It's deeper than that. Even the enemy knows God. It's time for war. This will not be an easy fight. Therefore, we must:

- Meditate on God with God. Fill your daily thoughts with God and on His character, His glory, majesty, love, goodness, grace, and mercy. Develop a contrite heart and spirit. (Psalm 8:1)
- Meditate on the Word in the Word. Get beyond books and get a Bible that you can read and understand. Purchase a good study Bible.

Set time aside to study the Word, ask questions, review passages, and look up Greek and Hebrew meanings.

- Meditate on self in the Word with God. Ask the Lord to show you yourself. Ask Him to expose your flaws and the inner secret of the workings of sin. Ask God to share with you what advantages the flesh has over you, what temptations it has used with success, what harm it has already caused, and what harm it still plans. Ask the Lord to shine a light in the dark areas of your mind and heart.

In my first book *Ready to Change My Name: A Spiritual Journey from Fear to Faith* I wrote:

The Bible says, "Then you will know the truth, and the truth will set you free" (John 8:32) and "Finally, brothers, whatever is true...think about such things." (Philippians 4:8) I'm tired of spending time on things that are not true, things that are not pure, not right, not noble or not lovely. The truth is in the Word of God. The truth is God's light. This truth will set you free. Look at it this way: truth equals freedom.

I'm tired of the bondage of lies, living in darkness and the hidden truth. We get caught up in living in the darkness of hearsay, assumptions, false information, and intentional lies, instead of truth. Start something new. Every time someone comes to you bringing information, ask them, "Is this the truth? Will this make me live in God's light or keep me in the darkness?" The next time you want to get out of something, don't lie. Tell the truth. When Satan whispers a lie, rebuke it and tell yourself the truth, God's truth. "And you will know the truth and the truth will set you free." Consider the words of Ephesians 4, "Live no longer as the ungodly do, for they are hopelessly confused. Their closed minds are full of darkness; they are far away from the life of God because they have shut their minds."

When you live in darkness, you are allowing Satan to have a hold on you. The truth gets lost in the darkness. This allows for confusion. Remain in God's light. In the darkness, Satan can keep his hands on you. He preys on your weaknesses, and it becomes easier for him when you are in the dark. Let it be known that Jesus alone has the power to bind the brokenhearted, set the captives free and release people from the prison of emotional, psychological, and spiritual darkness. And just knowing about the Lord is not enough when the shackles of life have you bound and overwhelmed in darkness. When we intimately experience and become consumed with our Lord and Savior Jesus Christ to find permanent freedom from this darkness, the shadows have no power in our lives.

As a recap, we need to examine the garbage in our thinking. Many of us are occupied with the things others plant into our minds. We must trust in the Lord with all our hearts and lean not unto our own understanding (Proverbs 3:5-6). Trust God. And let Him lead us into the light.

Now that you have completed this chapter ask yourself, "Who Told You That?"

And now you know...

GUARD YOUR CONVERSATION

One thing we do not always consider is the importance of guarding our conversation and understanding the motives of individuals we share information with. Can you remember any time that the Lord whispered into your spirit as you were talking to someone, "Don't share that." and still you kept talking, sharing something that later you wished you had not. I have, and many times wished that I had just been obedient. In reading Ephesians 2, "Wherein in time past ye walked according to the course of this world, according to the prince of the power of the air, the spirit that now worketh in the children of disobedience: Among whom also we all had our conversation in times past in the lusts of our flesh, fulfilling the desires of the flesh and of the mind; and were by nature the children of wrath, even as others" (Ephesians 2:2-3, KJV). The enemy is the prince of the power of the air. He takes the very things we put out in the universe, captures them and uses them against us. He is so crafty. He takes our information and creates deceit, causing confusion among people and creating false beliefs.

The devil is a liar. Jesus called him "a liar and the father of lies" (John 8:44, NLT). The Message Bible records it as following: "'If God were your father,' said Jesus, 'you would love me, for I came from God and arrived here. I didn't come on my own. He sent me. Why can't you understand one word I say? Here's why: You can't handle it. You're from your father, the Devil, and all you want to do is please him. He was a killer from the very start. He couldn't stand the truth because there wasn't a shred of truth in him. When the Liar speaks, he makes it up out of his lying nature and fills the world with lies. I arrive on the scene, tell you the plain truth, and you refuse to have a thing to do with me. Can any one of you convict me of a single misleading word, a single sinful act? But if I'm telling the truth, why don't you believe me? Anyone on God's side listens to God's words. This is why you're not listening—because you're not on a God's side'" (John 8:42-47, MSG).

The enemy comes to whisper things into our spirit that are far from the truth. He will tell us things that will get us to doubt ourselves, our potential, and will try to destroy our very soul. He comes to steal, kill and destroy (John 10:10), and oftentimes, we allow him to do just that: steal our dreams, kill our desires, and destroy our future. He comes to give us glimpses of truth, enabling us to twist it in our minds, and then let us damage ourselves by believing the lies. He tests us to see what we will do with the first bits of information he shares with us. The enemy gives us just enough to cause us to think about ending a friendship or relationship, not accepting a position, or not attempting to stretch ourselves towards a goal. We struggle with the lies that have been deposited into our spirit, and even if we push through those lies towards what God has for us, he lurks and attempts to finish us off. Again, the devil is a liar.

Looking back at Genesis 3, "The serpent was the shrewdest of all the wild animals the LORD God had made. One day he asked the woman, "Did God really say you must not eat the fruit from ANY of the trees in the garden?" (NLT). In Eugene Peterson's The Message, it reads, "The serpent was clever, more clever than any wild animal GOD had made. He spoke to the Woman: "Do I understand that God told you not to eat from ANY tree in the garden?"

The New Living Translation

"Really?" he asked the woman. "Did God really say that you must not eat…"

At this point the woman should have thought to herself, "What are the motives of the serpent?" We need to stop and think about our conversations and ask ourselves, "What is the motive?" of the other person. In asking this question, we may be able to see if the person is trying to gain something or if they are simply having a conversation with no agenda. If we doubt the intent even a moment, our conversation should be guarded. The Holy Spirit could be warning you. We see in Genesis 3 that the woman responds to the serpent. "Of course we may eat fruit from the trees in the garden." This is the point at which she should have stopped. In continuing on, she gave the serpent room to twist the truth. She continued on saying "It's only the fruit from the tree in the middle of the garden that we are not allowed to eat. God said 'You must not eat it or even touch it; if you do, you will die.'" Stop right here for a quick Bible lesson. Go back and reread the scripture of what God said carefully in, Genesis 3:17. God never said, "or even touch it" the woman added this herself to the conversation. No matter which translation you read, God never said, "touch." He said in Genesis 2:17, "but you must not eat from the tree of the knowledge of good and evil, for when you eat of it you will surely die." Notice He never said, "Touch." The woman is carrying on a conversation with the serpent that of course is the enemy and begins to add her own take and insert her own words to the truth. You see we too will distort the truth as we are trying to prove ourselves. More on this later in the chapter called "Holy Disguised."

One can only assume the enemy had been watching the woman for some time. He knew what to say to her, and he knew to some degree how she would respond. Basically, the enemy constructed a trap and she walked right into it when she opened her mouth. She began so well and was strong in her initial reply to the serpent. BUT . . . she continued to run her mouth. This is so like many of us. We want people to know the whole truth and nothing but the truth, and we want to be the ones to tell them about it! The question is "Why?" Why is it so important to us to prove that we know everything that is going on? Why is it so important to share with anyone and everyone what we know, even if there is truth in what we share? What is the point? And what do we hope to gain? Does it give us some sort of special status? Actually, what it does many times is put you and me in a place where our backs are up against the wall.

In Genesis 3:4, the serpent responds to the woman: "Surely you won't die." Many of us could translate this to "surely you won't get caught," or "surely no one will find out," or "surely you won't get too drunk or high." Then there is "surely you won't lose favor" or "surely you won't get pregnant" or "surely you won't..." You can fill in the blank. "Surely" does not have a face, but I have learned that "surely" can mess you up! We can think "surely, I should be able to share this information with..." and later find out that the information is not completely true and could potentially hurt someone. Because it is only a portion of truth, it is really a lie. Sprinkling your conversation with a little deceit makes the entire conversation an untruth. This is the enemy's snare. He will whisper a little deceit into the truth to get you to fall for something that isn't true. God said in the beginning, "It's good." When, then, did the woman allow the enemy to tell her something different? He plays on our insecurities, and giving us a sneak peek into the life of others, we put our own spin to the story based upon what we think we already know. Remember that the enemy approached the woman by saying, "Did God really say…?" This is what we do to each other. We say, "Did your husband really…?" "Did my boss really say…?" Did your wife really go…?" Did you really…?" You can fill in the blank. This is how it all gets started. It's a trick that we so easily fall into. The enemy lays out a well-thought plan and because we are not looking for it, we fall into the enemy's schemes and share more information than needed, leading to more drama in our lives.

Are you ready to believe the truth? How would you like to expose the truth in your life and get the enemy off your trail? You can confront the lies and speak the truth into your spirit. Yes, it is possible the enemy has your back up against the wall. It is possible that you can see the truth and then, suddenly, the enemy flees, but you are left with a mess on your hands. You are left with unresolved issues and find yourself unable to get out of the situation you have placed yourself in. The enemy can hide just out of reach, letting you rest long enough to think he was gone for good, then drop from nowhere back into your life and more specifically, your head, whispering those lies. Therein lies the advantage of the lies you have been told time and time again. This is the advantage of those conversations you have had where you opened your mouth and now question if you should have spoken those words out loud. It lurks in an unsearchable and deceitful fortress, where you can't find the very one who started these whispers of lies.

Ephesians 6:12

For our struggle is not against flesh and blood, but against the rulers, against the authorities, against the powers of this dark world and against the spiritual forces of evil in the heavenly realms.

Have you ever battled some of the lies or conversations you now wish you were never a part of—prayed and fasted and sought counsel against your part in it? You thought the conversation was over and done with. You thought you were able to move past it. Then, one day you find yourself involved in a group conversation and what you previously shared is brought up. Only this time it is twisted and has taken a turn. You realize that you have shared way too much information and now realize that you fell for the enemy's trap. You know those trick birthday candles that light up even after they have been blown out? Your conversations can be just like those candles. They never go out but keep relighting over and over again. James 3:6 says, "The tongue also is a fire, a world of evil among the parts of the body. It corrupts the whole body, sets the whole course of one's life on fire, and is itself set on fire by hell." We must learn to guard our conversations.

A word of caution: NEVER think for a moment that the war against the enemy is over. Remember that we do not wrestle against flesh and blood, but against principalities, against powers, against the rulers of darkness of this age, against spiritual hosts of wickedness to the heavenly places (see Ephesians 6:12).

Know this: YOU ARE RESCUED FROM THE PIT OF THE ENEMY'S SCHEMES—TODAY!

Guard your conversations. Remember to ask yourself: *"Who told you that?"*

GUARD YOUR HEART AND MIND

People can be brutal. Have you ever found yourself in a conversation that you did not request? People begin to give you information on how to live your life although you never asked them a question. I have; I recall a time during a "girls' night out" and all of a sudden, a mother of a friend of mine said, "You need to change your image." I continued to do what I was doing because there was no way she was speaking to me. She tapped me on the shoulder and said, "Did you hear me? You need to change your image." I thought I would indulge her for a moment to hear what she had to say. Bottom line, she did not like the fact that every time she saw me, I was dressed in blue jeans. Proverbs 4:23 says, "Above all else, guard your heart, for everything you do flows from it." The first thing I needed to do was guard my heart.

A few weeks later while speaking with the daughter of the woman who suggested that I change my image, the daughter said to me, "Why did you tell my mom that you were grown and therefore did not appreciate her suggestion of looking at another designer for purchasing your jeans?" Of course, I asked, "Who Told You That?" and I began to explain the conversation. No matter what I said, my friend "told" me what I did say. I find it interesting that you can say one thing, but because a portion of what was said is turned around or left out the entire thing is turned into a lie. I thought; how dare you tell me what I said when in fact I did not.

The Bible tells us in Philippians 4:7, "And the peace of God, which transcends all understanding, will guard your hearts and your minds in Christ Jesus." How shall we guard our minds? It is possible to allow our mind to run rampant. The mind will direct you one way as it follows the heart. Our heart must be right with God. In the above story of the daughter and her mother, it was imperative that I guard both my heart and my mind. It is easy to try to defend oneself, but the truth is they have their minds made up what they already believe. The best thing you can do is to guard your heart.

We come face to face with the enemy within. "For if you live according to the sinful nature [flesh], you will die; but if by the Spirit you put to death the misdeeds of the body, you will live" (Romans 8:13). The best thing we can do when faced with this situation is to trust in the Lord will all of our heart, mind, and strength and to allow the Lord our God to decrease our flesh. Our flesh wants nothing more than to rise to the top and have a quick reaction to respond to nonsense. But since it is nonsense, we must guard our heart and mind and rely on the strength we have in the Spirit that lives within us.

God has given us His Word, the Holy Bible, as a tool. However, to the flesh's enchantment, most Christians are ignorant of the power the Lord has handed to each of us, His children. He has also given us access and the keys to the kingdom, but for many of us we try to use keys for a Honda for keys to a Mercedes. For others, they have lost the keys. Some of us attack the attacker and spiritually die in the process. Others sit in the shadow of the attacker out of fear. And yet others become stifled under the grip of the enemy afraid for their life until fear ends up crushing the very life we have been ordained to live. 2 Timothy 1:7 says, "For God did not give us a spirit of timidity, but a spirit of power, of love and of self-discipline"

The flesh, thought, will, and emotions work by deceit and the primary target is the mind. If the enemy is successful in getting to you through your mind it will affect your heart as well. This is how our heart becomes hardened. If the mind gives in—well, it's over. We have to guard our heart and mind. To protect oneself against the mind's deceit, we have to fix our mind on the love of Jesus. Here is our dilemma: the flesh resists with all its strength, therefore, we must rely solely on Christ to prevent being lied to and tricked in the first place.

Let us look at Romans 7:15-20 NIV:

¹⁵ I do not understand what I do. For what I want to do I do not do, but what I hate I do. ¹⁶ And if I do what I do not want to do, I agree that the law is good. ¹⁷ As it is, it is no longer I myself who do it, but it is sin living in me. ¹⁸ For I know that good itself does not dwell in me, that is, in my sinful nature. For I have the desire to do what is good, but I cannot carry it out. ¹⁹ For I do not do the good I want to do, but the evil I do not want to do — this I keep on doing. ²⁰ Now if I do what I do not want to do, it is no longer I who do it, but it is sin living in me that does it.

If our mind gives in to what is of the flesh — well, it's over. It never fails. We say we want to stop complaining, but the moment we make that acknowledgment we complain more than ever. It appears that our tongue will do nothing but complain. We find we are complaining more after we make the vow than we have in our entire lifetime. We desire to do well, but for whatever reason we are unable to do well. Here's the real issue: we rely on our own strength when we should rely solely upon the Lord.

We believe we can solve our own problem by reading and praying as a habit. Forming a habit will not help us. We must give of ourselves totally and completely to Christ and be mindful of building a deep and intimate love relationship with Him. As I shared in the chapter "It's Made Up," I would like to reiterate that we try to get by with saying, "I've read a scripture this morning" but reading a scripture has nothing to do with living the scripture you have read. Saying, "The Lord is my Shepherd" does not mean that you know the Shepherd. Saying, "Now I lay me down to sleep" will not constitute that you will rest well. It's deeper than that.

We have to seek the Lord with all our heart, trust in the Lord, and lean not to our own understanding (Proverbs 3:5). I have listed again the steps to grow deeper in the Lord:

1. Take time with God and His Word. Fill your thoughts with the thoughts of God, His character, glory, majesty, love, goodness, grace, and mercy. Be in relationship with Him. Get to know Him. Believe God. Submit yourself to God. Humble yourself to Him. Have a repentant heart and spirit. (Psalm 8:1)

2. Meditate on the Word of God day and night. Know His Word. Set time aside to study God's Word, ask questions, look up passages, read the Bible in different translations to get an understanding. Live the Word of God.

3. Ask the Lord for revelation knowledge as you are reading the Word of the Lord. Ask Him to expose your flaws and the inner secret of the workings of sin. Ask God to share with you what advantages the flesh has over you, what temptations it has used with success, what harm it has already caused, and what harm it

still plans. Ask the Lord to shine a light in the dark areas of your mind and heart.

When these three suggestions are implemented, someone like the daughter and her mother that you read about in the beginning of the chapter will not bother you. You will realize you are wasting time defending yourself. It's not worth it. You will know the truth and the truth will set you free. You will live a life of freedom and your heart and mind will be guarded because you have the Word of the Lord within you.

So ask yourself, "Who Told You That?"

And now you know…

DON'T BRING OTHERS IN

God is amazing. He comes bearing the truth. He even gives us a way out of our burdens. "Come to me, all you who are weary and burdened, and I will give you rest. Take my yoke upon you and learn from me, for I am gentle and humble in heart, and you will find rest for your souls. For my yoke is easy and my burden is light" (Matthew 11:28-30). For some reason, we do the opposite of what God says and do not take Jesus up on His offer. Let's look back at the woman in Genesis 3 who spoke with the serpent. Eve listened to the serpent. She saw that the fruit of the tree was good for food and pleasing to the eye and also desirable for gaining wisdom. She went a step further and decided to pull her husband into her disobedience and he ate with her. It is one thing if you decide to follow the crowd doing the wrong thing. It is quite another if you are leading the pack.

As long as Eve could see things clearly, she was fine. But when the serpent deceived her, she ate (Genesis 3:13). Trickery has always been and always will be Satan's way of operating. Here's a word of caution: never allow someone else to entice you to fall into the enemy's traps of deception. Don't allow your mind to take you on a road trip. And don't pull others into his traps with you. Eve pulled in Adam. It made her culpable.

The woman sinned by choice. The serpent did not tell her to sin. She made the decision to disobey God on her own based on her information in front of her. Her choice. It is truly easy to get caught up. Before you realize it, your mind has taken a road trip and now you find you are in too deep and don't know how to get out of the situation. How many of us look at the temptation in front of us and say to ourselves, "well, I know I'm not supposed to do this, but it sure looks like I would enjoy it. It can't really be that bad for me." The consequences are always more than we bargained for because disobedience costs.

Ask yourself, "How can I prevent myself from falling into the traps of deception? How can I become more aware of the enemy's tricks? Why do I continue to get caught up in idle chit-chat? What is it about me? What am I looking for? When I'm in conversation with others, who is talking and to whom am I responding? Am I trusting God and listening to Him or am I trying to handle this all on my own?"

In order to prevent yourself from falling into the trap of deception, you must understand and believe in what is true and believe God. Notice that I didn't say believe IN God, but believe God. There is a difference. Even the enemy believes in God. How many of us actually choose to believe what God says in His Word?

Let's take a look at another woman in the Bible, Sarai. Genesis 16 begins, "Now Sarai, Abram's wife, had borne him no children. But she had an Egyptian maidservant named Hagar; so she said to Abram, 'The LORD has kept me from having children. Go, sleep with my maidservant; perhaps I can build a family through her.' Abram agreed to what Sarai said." (Genesis 16:1-2) Sarai was older and believed that she would not bear children. God wasn't working fast enough for her so she took matters into her own hands, using Hagar to build her family. Sound familiar? She made the decision to pull her maidservant into her mess.

As you can imagine, when Hagar knew she was pregnant, she began to "trip." Sarai began to blame Abram. Remember, he only did what she told him to do! After her presumed pouting, complaining, and probable nagging, Abram told Sarai, "Your servant is in your hands." Bad move. Hagar fled and even more confusion was created. Sarai pulled Hagar in to get what she wanted. It's no different from what we do today. When things aren't going as planned, what do we do? We look to see who we can complain to, cry to, pout to. We see who we can get to side with us so we feel justified in our mess. Don't believe me? What do you do when you are looking for a raise and are afraid that your boss won't listen to you or support you? What about when your spouse isn't doing what you want him or her to do? What do you do when you feel you need reinforcement or backup? You find a "friend" who will tell you what you want to hear or get involved in the situation to "fix" it. What is this really called? It is manipulation. We'll talk more about that in another chapter. I love the words of Joyce Meyer, who says in her book *Battlefield of the Mind*, Satan could inject thoughts into your mind. "Much of what was in my head was either lies that Satan was telling me or just plain nonsense—things that really were not worth spending my time thinking about. The devil was controlling my life because he was controlling my thoughts." You see, the devil will sneak in and begin to control your thoughts and before you know it, you will have pulled others into your thinking. You need backup and you will take any prisoner hostage as long as you get what you want.

We see what happens later to Sarah. In Genesis 18, we see where Sarah lies to God. *"Now Sarah was listening at the entrance to the tent, which was behind him. . . . So Sarah laughed to herself as she thought, "After I am worn out and my master is old, will I now have this pleasure?"* (18:10-12). In verse 15 we find that Sarah lies to God, claiming that she has not laughed. God confronts her with her lie and says to Sarah, *"Yes, you did laugh."* Sarah was unable to believe the truth, even after God eventually blessed her with a son. She pulled Hagar into her scheme and caused more drama rather than believing and waiting on God. God, however, will always confront you with the truth. We have to be willing to hear it.

Each one of us needs someone in our lives who loves us enough to confront us with truth. We need someone who can knock us back into our right minds and wake us up so we don't believe all the lies around us and fall into the enemy's traps. Remember Nathan in the book of Samuel? Nathan confronted David who was attempting to place blame on someone else for his wrongdoing. Nathan called him out saying, "You are the man!" (2 Samuel 12:7). Trying to blame someone else for your errors will always lead to more chaos and pain. It is another way that the enemy pulls us away from God. We are to take accountability for ourselves and not pull others into our mess. Remember Nehemiah? Four times they sent him a message to get him off track, and four times he sent the same message back. Nehemiah did not pull anyone else; he did not waver. He didn't add any additional information. Nehemiah never explained himself. He simply did what he was called to do based upon the truth. Others around him came to him with lies, but he stood on the truth of the Lord. His faith was never shaken and never was the enemy successful in distracting him.

In order not to pull others into your mess, accept responsibility for those things you allow yourself to get into. Even when you find yourself in a "pickle," be accountable. Pick yourself up, dust yourself off, and learn from your mistakes.

It's made up. Guard your conversation. Don't pull others into your mess.

Remember to ask, "Who told you that?"
And now you know…

WHO TOLD YOU THAT?

Anytime I speak or write, I tend to be transparent. As I begin writing this chapter, I want to share a "transparent moment," setting the stage to set someone free.

As I sit and reflect over my life, I recall the times when I allowed the enemy to have the upper hand in my life. There have been moments throughout the last year when I was preparing to preach or teach the Gospel of Jesus that the enemy whispered to me, "Don't preach that message." These are the times after I have allowed the enemy to harass me that I simply want to give up. Yelling, "I quit!" I want to throw in the towel because I have allowed the enemy in to tell me that what I am doing is not working.

I have questioned my life purpose. I have doubted God and the calling He has placed on my life. I have questioned God. All because I have given access to the enemy, allowing him to whisper lies into my being.

Many times, God sends me messages and warnings through dreams. You see, God has gifted me to dream dreams and to see visions. It never fails—the enemy will try to distract me or stop me from delivering a message that will crush him with one strike of my heel (Genesis 3:15). I recall a dream I had about a little boy knocking at my door, and when I opened it, the little boy started sharing a concern with me. I bent down to help him, and as I bent, a giant appeared in the little boy's place and began to force his way toward me. This dream was God preparing me for what the enemy was throwing my way. The only thing I knew was that the characters were in reverse. The little boy was actually the giant, and the giant was the one being used by the deceiver. The giant got caught up by the deceiver's lies and was being used. The devil comes to steal, kill and destroy (John 10:10), and anytime we open the door, we allow the enemy to steal our passion, kill our desire, or destroy what God has called us to. We must remember the rest of the scripture, "Jesus comes that we may have life and have it to the full." So I ask, "Who are you going to listen to?" You decide. Believe the truth of the Lord or the lie of the enemy. It's your choice. We must ask, "Who told you that?"

I am not the only one who has been in this place. I know you are either at this crossroad or have been at this crossroad at some point during your life. For whatever reason, you may be feeling undervalued, incompetent, ill-equipped, unappreciated, undeserving, not good enough, unworthy, and overlooked in your job, community, your local church, at your children's school, and yes, even in your own home. Quiet your spirit. What you are experiencing is the reason God chose you!

I wonder sometimes if I am capable and equipped to do the work that has been given to me. As another may question my ability, I begin to question myself. Here's a question for us to ask ourselves: Why are we looking to others to give us the approval that God has already given to us? This is exactly what the enemy wants for you and me to do. This is his setup, for us to begin to doubt and fall prey to his lies.

When we begin to question and to look back over our life, Satan plants doubt and gives us a rewind based upon previous roadblocks, showing us our potential to ruin the assignment God has given to you and me. Fear and worry consume our mind and control our behavior. I have come to the conclusion that many of us are insecure, full of fear, scared of the unknown, double-minded, self-centered, and perhaps people-pleasers. This is why we are unsure of the calling that has been placed upon us. When we get to this point, it's only by the grace of God that we don't lose our mind. Have you ever had people question your calling? Have you ever had anyone ask you why you do the things you do? They were not convinced that God really called you. They tried everything possible to turn you away. They interrogated you. They recalled your past to discourage you from continuing. They zone in on all the reasons why you cannot and should not do what you believe to be "the call" the Lord has placed upon your heart. They have reminded you of your mistakes and shortcomings. These very questions put you in a posture of feeling less-than and discouraged about moving forward. Is it because we are operating in a spirit of fear of the unknown that we struggle with moving forward? Has it crossed your mind that Satan himself is harassing you? Is he putting reasons in front of you as to why you should stay under his yoke of bondage? Has it ever crossed your mind that the people who are trying to discourage you are the very ones who are being used by the enemy? Allow me to whisper in your ear a word that could free you. Those people do not know that they are being used. Don't get mad at them—realize it is all a trick that the enemy is using for your demise. It's a lie. It's a trick!

I have walked into a room of people and felt that no one wanted me around. This could be a sign the enemy is whispering lies into your ear. I have been in situations when the Lord has specifically called me to an assignment; however, others at the table begin to criticize and will tell me how best to do something or question whether I should do it at all. I have had to learn that it is the enemy who is trying to get me to step aside. He is trying to get you off track as well. Don't fall for his tricks and his lies. Quitting appears to be easy, but you know that God has charged you with an assignment that cannot be avoided.

I want to share something important with you. **Man did not choose you—God did!** The Bible declares in John 15:16, "You did not choose me, but I chose you and appointed you so that you might go and bear fruit — fruit that will last — and so that whatever you ask in my name the Father will give you." Therefore, since God chose you, why do you sit and struggle with the lies that have been spoken into your spirit? Why struggle with your day-to-day activities? Why struggle with who you are in Christ? I will tell you, we struggle because somewhere in our upbringing, we were lied to, and for some, we are continually lied to and told that to make it in this world, we have to please everyone. Where did that lie come from? It was a subtle lie whispered in our ear that said we should say "yes" to everything that was asked of us. It was the kind of lie telling us that if we want to make it in this game called life, we needed to be available at all times. It was the sort of lie we told ourselves in order to be liked by everyone, but found out later they still didn't like us. We were only being used.

So now we struggle. We struggle because we are not sure how to come out from under the lie that became a part of our lives. We're ready to do something new and to step into our calling to find ourselves seeking validation from everyone but God. We are trying to position ourselves to serve within a leadership role but struggle with the lies that have been spoken. We believe that no one is listening because of our history that the enemy so cleverly reminds us of. Hush. Quiet the pounding of your heart and the voices of your head. Surrender to God and walk in obedience to all He has called you to. I encourage you to stay true to who Christ has wonderfully made you to be. Stop believing the lies of the enemy.

As I continue to stay transparent, another challenge for me is when the Lord tells me to be silent. There are times when He does not give me permission to expose the truth. There are times when I am angry with God for not allowing me to tell people what is really going on. Ever wanted to clear your name? I have and could have cleared my name many times, but God will tell me to be still and know that He is God (Psalm 46:10). I suppose the Lord would have me experience a little of what Nehemiah experienced. Nehemiah doesn't even address the enemy for two chapters. We must remember in situations where we are lied about, put down, or persecuted, the Lord redeems us in His time and in His way. There are times when I would still like to say something! God has already fought and won this victory. However, notice that when Nehemiah does respond, it is short and sweet. His response in today's terms would be something like "Okay. Whatever. Now go away. I have work to do."

Again, here are some questions to ask yourself when you are dealing with others.

- How can I prevent falling into the trap of deception?
- How can I prevent being tricked by the enemy?
- Why do I get caught up in idle conversations?
- Who are we responding to?

- Are you responding to the lies and tricks of the enemy?
- Are you resolving issues on your own, or are you trusting God and His direction?

We must learn to ask ourselves the question, "Who told you that?" I have had to learn to ask, what does this person who is saying these things have to lose, and what do I have to gain? Remember that the devil is a liar and he is seeking someone to devour! I love the way Nehemiah replied to the messenger in Nehemiah 6. He said to Sanballat, "You know you are lying, there's no truth in any part of your story" (NLT). No different from how the Lord told Sarah that she lied. It's time to confront some of this mess when God says it is okay to confront. Ask yourself and others, "Who told you that?"

Back in Genesis, Adam and the woman heard the sound of the Lord God, so they went and hid. When God called out to Adam and said, "Where are you?" it was not that God didn't know where they were. He knows everything. He asked them for a reason. When Adam responded that they were naked, God asked, "Who told you that?" Oh, my! He has set me up to make my point.

Notice earlier that Adam and the woman were not ashamed (Genesis 2:25).

Notice that the serpent disappeared after he started all of this mess.

Let's talk about sin consequence.

The Lord God confronts Adam and He confronts the woman. What happened then? The finger-pointing began. Isn't it amazing that once you have been caught, you begin to play the blame game? Adam blames the woman, and the woman points her finger at the serpent. She said *"the serpent deceived me, and I ate."* That is similar to what we say when we've been caught. "Well, that person lied to me and then I went for it. But it wasn't really my fault."

The Lord God started with the serpent and said, *"Because you have done this, you are cursed! Cursed to crawl on your belly and eat dirt all the rest of your life!"* In The Message Bible, the Lord God said to the serpent *"I'm declaring war between you and the Woman! . . . He'll wound your head ,. you'll wound his heel."* Then the Lord God says to the woman, *"I will greatly increase your pains in childbearing."* To Adam, He says, *"Because you listened to your wife – cursed is the ground because of you."*

Because of the lie and the disobedience, there was consequence. Because of deceit, there was pain.

Let's go back to the question, the title of this chapter, "Who Told You That?" Look at the following questions and answer them for yourself.

- Who told you that you were never going to make it? Who told you that?
- Who told you that you would never amount to anything? Who told you that?

- Who told you that you would be single the rest of your life? Who told you that?
- Who told you that you were unsuccessful? Who told you that?
- Who told you that she was talking about you? Who told you that?
- Who told you that you didn't deserve happiness, joy, and peace? Who told you that?
- Who told you that you weren't beautiful? Who told you that?
- Who told you that you weren't loved? Who told you that?

_____

_____

_____

_____

_____

_____

_____

_____

_____

_____

_____

_____

_____

Again, learn how to confront the lie like Nehemiah confronted Sanballat in Nehemiah 6:8, "You know you are lying, there's no truth in any part of your story" (NLT).

Do you remember back when we were young and we would sing, "Liar, liar, pants on fire?" It's time to take the lies that have been told to you or that you have been telling yourself and cast them into the pit of hell where they belong. I remember my husband preaching a sermon when he said, "Tell hell—NO!" It's time that we tell hell no, and it's time to put those lies where they belong. It is time to believe the truth of God.

Right now is the beginning of the rest of your life! Because of who you are through Jesus Christ, you can speak the truth and say…

- I am more than a conqueror.
- I am the head and not the tail.
- I am the child of the Most High God.
- I am a child of the King.
- I am a son of Abraham.
- I am a daughter of Zion.
- I am delivered.
- I am healed.
- I am free.
- I am walking in the authority of Christ Jesus.
- I am in my right mind.
- I am …you fill in the blank.

And now you know…

dARe

WHERE IS MY VOICE?

I dare you to speak up in church as a woman. I double dare you! We are all very familiar with 1 Corinthians 14:34-35, "Women should remain silent in the churches. They are not allowed to speak, but must be in submission, as the law says. If they want to inquire about something, they should ask their own husbands at home; for it is disgraceful for a woman to speak in the church." This passage of scripture has been used to try and silence women in the church. Here's the truth about the lie that has been told one too many times to try to silence women in the church today. Paul was correcting the church of Corinth because they had lost focus of the foundation of Christ. People in the church were speaking out of turn and doing their own thing. It's interesting how we pull out verse 34 and 35 and forget about reading the beginning of the section titled, "Orderly Worship" in the NIV Bible which begins at verse 26. Now, what's really important to get the full understanding is to read verse 36 which begins with, "Did the word of God originate with you?"

Paul was correcting the church. He used verse 26 to 35 to make his point.

I know I have a voice but sometimes wonder where my voice is as I have listened to people deposit lie after lie into my spirit. In writing this book I learned quickly how many other people felt this way too after I conducted an informal survey and received 97 responses. What I heard and the questions their responses ignited in me are sampled below.

- "Teachers told me growing up 'you will not be as good as your older brothers and sisters.' Now maybe that is true that I am not as good as them, but the truth is, did the teacher really know this? How did the teacher arrive at this answer?" Where is the voice of the respondent? Did she ask her teacher the question? More than likely, she didn't ask the question because many of us were taught not to question authority figures.
- "My dad told me 'Girls should not go to college; it's a waste of money.'" This woman's mother died when she was three years old. I wonder what her mother might have said.
- "'You are my best friend,' my best friend assured me as she was betraying my trust with my boyfriend."
- "My stepsister called me a 'Little Bitch' when it wasn't commonly heard. As I look back,

I can say that I have never in my life been a female dog!"

- "'I won't go any further...' promised my boy-friend. He did."

- "'You can trust me with this information. I won't tell anyone else.' A friend promised this to me as she told everything to everyone else."

- "'You have disappointed me.' I guess this is not a lie, but hurtful enough to make me want to prove I can do something with my life. It was so freeing to me later in life when God let me know that He was not disappointed in me. He knew exactly what I would do and He still loves me."

- "All my friends are getting married. If I don't soon, I will be an "Old Maid." This is what I felt and ended up getting married. I was 20 years old."

- "I thought submission to my husband would be easy because I love him so much."

- "My house must be perfect for my husband."

- "I should keep silent in an argument."

- "I can lie about how I feel during an argument to keep the peace."

- "I really need to purchase these things so I can be accepted."

- "My parents thought other people's children were perfect. What was wrong with me?"

Let's stop here for a moment and talk about a few of these responses, a few of the lies that were whispered into these respondents' spirits. Allow me to work backward through the quotes.

"What was wrong with me?" I often hear parents today point out to their children to look at the other children to see how well behaved they are and how those children are doing so well. This really makes my skin boil! Do parents realize that they are, by comparing their children, sending the message that their own children are not good enough? I can remember a specific example of this when my own daughter was three and being cared for by a woman out of her home. I remember walking in to pick up my daughter at the end of the day and when I walked in, I saw all of these pictures the children had painted hung up around the room. My daughter was so excited to show me her work. I applauded her and told her how beautifully she had painted. I remember even calling her a genius! She was so pleased and you could see the pride all over her face. Now, seriously, I have absolutely no idea what the picture was; she was only three! But all that mattered was that she was proud of it, and I wanted her to see how proud I was of her. Then, another mom came in. Her son ran up to her with his artwork and her response was a flat, "What is it? You painted outside of the lines. Why couldn't you do what the other kids did? We'll have to work with you to do better." I remember wanting to scream, I was so angry with this woman. I turned to see her son drop his head and rip

74

up his artwork. I reached out and said to him, "Your art-work is very creative. Don't rip it up anymore. Let's get some tape and we'll put it back together. I would love to display your work." I didn't lie to either child. I encouraged them. I didn't compare them. What was important was that they knew that they were their own individual people with their own unique personalities and talents. It didn't matter what they had painted. It was their work and creativity and the pride they had in their abilities that mattered.

"I really need to purchase these things so I can be accepted." This lie will send you immediately into debt, especially if you cannot afford the purchases. Furthermore, having things will not make people accept you. So often, people will live their lives to please others and soon find that there is nothing you can do to please everyone. Either they like you or they don't. Don't believe that what you have will really make a difference.

"I can lie about how I feel during an argument to keep the peace." What peace? This lie will send you to your death. Doctors share all the time that stress is the number one killer. So many people walk around with all these emotions and stress locked up on the inside and are sending their bodies into a slow death. How can you look for peace if you are keeping your feelings locked inside? Every time you are experiencing a confrontation, all those previous arguments that did not get resolved will bubble right back up. This is baggage. Brother, sister, express your thoughts and emotions. Express them with wisdom and in love, but do not keep it locked inside. The Bible calls us to speak the truth in love (Ephesians 4:15) and to not allow the sun to go down while you are angry (Ephesians 4:26). If we make the choice to stay silent or lie about how we feel, we are killing ourselves literally and choosing to live a lie.

You already know that these are all lies the enemy is speaking into your spirit. The people who are telling you these lies are only being used by the enemy. Let's look at what the Word of God says: "Then Jesus asked him, 'What is your name?' 'My name is Legion,' he replied, 'for we are many'" (Mark 5:9). Here was a man who was being used by Legion. I wonder how many people get so caught up in their own lack of self that they say anything to discourage other people. So often, when people say negative or hurtful things, we know somewhere in our spirit that these things are not true. But then, where is our voice to speak up and say, "No, that is not who I am?" We have allowed so many to speak into our situations and into our lives. Why can't we find the strength or develop a healthy self-esteem to let our own voices be heard? Is there something wrong with you or me? No. There is nothing wrong with you. You were taught early on, just like I was, that you accept what others, especially those in authority, have said to you. It's a learned behavior.

Ask yourself the following questions.

- How can you be a witness to someone else when you haven't been delivered yourself?

- How can you speak life to another when you speak death to yourself?
- What was said about your past? Your pain? Your childhood that keeps you holding on to the lies that were told to you?
- It's time to get over it. What are you going to do?

One of the questions I asked on the survey was "What lies has the enemy told you to try and distract you? One of the most common responses out of 97 individuals was "I am not valuable." How did we ever get to the point where we feel like we are not valuable? How have so many people fallen for this lie? When you go back to the beginning, as God created He said, "It is good." If all of His creations are good, and biblically speaking, He said it was so, then why do we feel like we are not? God sent His Son to die for you and me. If we were not valuable I do not believe God would have given His only begotten son, Jesus Christ, to die on a cross for us (John 3:16). Jesus said, "Not my will, but thy will be done!" (Matthew 26:42) Jesus gave up the ghost (Luke 23:46), and hung His head and died. Praise His holy name! Jesus rose with all power in His hands for me and for you! That's love and that is the truth, the whole truth and nothing but the truth! Read the account for yourself: John 19:1 through chapter 20:9.

I dare you to use your voice. I double dare you to believe the truth of the Lord and begin to speak and live all that God has spoken into your life. Isaiah 44:6 says,

"Thus saith the LORD the King of Israel, and his redeemer the LORD of hosts; I am the first, and I am the last; and beside me there is no God" (KJV).

Here's a question for you, "Who Told You That?" Who told you not to use your voice?

Who Told You That?

And now you know…

Please Do Not Try to Silence Me

How many times have we tried to silence someone or been silenced ourselves? I cannot count the times somebody has tried to keep me quiet. It began early in elementary school. I was, and am, a talker. I did not wait until the teacher called on me. I would raise my hand and before she would call my name, I would call out the answer. Additionally, I would talk to every other student in the classroom just because I wanted to. I was always in the principal's office, always in trouble for talking. I would come home after school only to be disciplined again for talking. I would get in trouble with other people for talking. I was going to talk, and people were always trying their best to get me to stop, to silence me. I had something to say and people were always telling me to be quiet. We find the same sort of thing happening to a blind man, Bartimaeus, in the Book of Luke.

³⁵ As Jesus approached Jericho, a blind man was sitting by the roadside begging. ³⁶ When he heard the crowd going by, he asked what was happening. ³⁷ They told him, "Jesus of Nazareth is passing by."

³⁸ He called out, "Jesus, Son of David, have mercy on me!"

³⁹ Those who led the way rebuked him and told him to be quiet, but he shouted all the more, "Son of David, have mercy on me!"

⁴⁰ Jesus stopped and ordered the man to be brought to him. When he came near, Jesus asked him, ⁴¹ "What do you want me to do for you?"

"Lord, I want to see," he replied.

⁴² Jesus said to him, "Receive your sight; your faith has healed you." ⁴³ Immediately he received his sight and followed Jesus, praising God. When all the people saw it, they also praised God. (Luke 18:35-43)

"Those who led the way rebuked him and told him to be quiet." I love it that Bartimaeus shouted all the more! Bartimaeus was probably thinking, "I need Jesus to hear me. I need to ask him to do something for me." Imagine if the individuals who were leading the way were able to silence blind Bartimaeus. This is what happens every time someone interferes with our life and tries to silence you and me. What are we missing out on once we have been silenced? Bartimaeus kept shouting and Jesus was able to hear him above the crowd and respond, "'What do you want me to do for you?' Bartimeus said, 'I want to see.'" Because he was not silent, he received his sight.

It is time for you and me to speak up and ask God what we will. If it lines up with what the Lord has for us, we will receive.

In studying young women and women of color, it is noted that we drift toward silence in corporate America, as well as within the community and education systems. We are living in the twenty-first century with legal equal rights. However, educated and seemingly confident young women and women of color, when dealing with men and Caucasian women choose to be silent versus risk rejection or dismissal by speaking up. We may question how that is possible or even disagree that this is happening today, but throughout my research it is evident that intimidation, degradation, disrespect, and condescension are used to keep young women and women of color from expressing their ideas or opinions. These tactics cause these women to take the safer route of silence time and time again.

Lisa Graham McMinn, associate professor of sociology at George Fox University, wrote in her book *Growing Strong Daughters*, "Women seem to have no confidence in their ability to learn or comprehend, and they depend entirely on others to direct them." Furthermore, McMinn states, "These girls are often raised in isolated homes. Not much talking occurred in their homes, and when it did, daughters more often heard hurtful words rather than nurturing ones." This leads me to wonder if we are silenced very early in life and carry that silence with us as we mature. Is there a lack of confidence in our girls that contributes to silencing their voices? Reading a line from *Women's Ways of Knowing*, it is noted that, "To a large extent, these perspectives were influenced by the homes girls grew up in."

In talking with some of my daughter's teenage friends, I learned that girls, unlike boys, will show that they are intimidated based on their upbringing. I asked several questions and learned that there is a sense of fear, a lack of confidence, a lack of respect, and overall silence with others unless they are prompted or encouraged to speak. One common factor was that many of the teenage girls, who are successful in school, indicated that they were taught at home to be quiet. The phrase I hear often is that they were taught to "speak only when spoken to." I think about when I was growing up. That was the household rule then as well. "Children are to be seen and not heard." Does this teaching continue to carry over in our homes and with our young women today? Does this "rule" continue into adulthood? Do we continue this learned behavior in the church?

Referring back to the survey I mentioned in the chapter, "Where Is My Voice?" I asked questions about church relationships. This is what was shared in the survey:

- "I was taught that Christians never gossiped. So when I was pulled into conversations by the older women in the church, I believed it was okay to share in the conversation."

- "It wasn't until later in life I learned that there were lies told in the church, about church, and about being a Christian. When I wanted to weigh in on a conversation, I was told to be quiet. Instead of using my voice, I made the decision to remain silent."
- "When I began to openly praise God during worship, I was pulled aside and told, 'You are not holy enough to praise God.' This quote broke my heart. Who would silence someone in the church? I have the answer: many people!

Here are some questions for you to consider. Take a moment to consider your past experiences with the church and outside of it.

Has anyone ever tried to silence you and your praise?

_____

_____

_____

Have you been deceived in the past by individuals in your local church? Explain.

_____

_____

_____

_____

How have you been lied to in the church or by other Christians? If so, how did that make you feel?

_____

_____

_____

What are you going to do to make your voice heard? How will you deal with individuals who try to silence you?

_____

_____

_____

How will you continue on this path of a speaking up and shouting all the more?

_____

_____

_____

Here is a scripture that is dear to my heart and one that has helped me when the enemy tries to speak lies into my spirit.

Finally, brothers and sisters, whatever is true, whatever is noble, whatever is right, whatever is pure, whatever is lovely, whatever is admirable — if anything is excellent or praiseworthy — think about such things.

Philippians 4:8

And then, in The Message Bible, it reads,

Summing it all up, friends, I'd say you'll do best by filling your minds and meditating on things true, noble, reputable, authentic, compelling, gracious — the best, not the worst; the beautiful, not the ugly; things to praise, not things to curse. Put into practice what you learned from me, what you heard and saw and realized. Do that, and God, who makes everything work together, will work you into his most excellent harmonies.

Philippians 4:8-9

Who Told You That you had to be silent? I dare you to use your voice. I double dare you.

And now you know...

EMOTIONS: OUT OF CONTROL

Ready to fight! Are you SURE? How would you like to fight an enemy who, just when you had him out of your mind, he dropped another lie into your spirit? It never fails. You have his back up against the wall, but then he hides himself into the night. An enemy who could hide just out of reach, letting you rest long enough to think he was gone for good, then drop from nowhere filling your head with a lie — nonsense that you don't know whether to believe or not. This is why it is so important to know the truth. The enemy lurks around, coming in and out, speaking lies into your spirit to the point where your emotions are out of control. You try to justify why you feel the way you feel, but the enemy has a grip on you and your mind. You try to get understanding, but he is so crafty and becomes unsearchable in his deceitful fortress, where you can't find him. Thinking of Genesis 3 where Adam blamed the woman and the woman blamed the serpent, but the serpent was nowhere to be found. Imagine that!

Have you ever battled some sort of addiction—then decided to attend church, received a quick lesson on praying and fasting, you even sought counsel, purchased a tape on deliverance—then watched it creep away into the night? You thought you had crushed this issue, but one day you were watching television, and a commercial for an upcoming series displayed a man without his shirt, built with a six-pack, tearing off the skirt of a woman, and it brought back every feeling of lust you had tried to overcome on your own. Sin can be like trick birthday candles: you make a wish and blow them out, but very soon there are flames once more. You're told that you can simply follow a few steps and conquer this on your own. Your emotions are out of control. The enemy is so slick that he tells you it's alright to watch the series with sexual content although you have a sex addiction. The devil is a liar! Send him back to the pit of hell when he belongs.

"We wrestle not against flesh and blood, but against principalities, against powers, against the rulers of darkness of this world, against spiritual wickedness in high places." (Ephesians 6:12, KJV) When we try to battle the enemy on our own, frankly we lose. We need Jesus to fight the battle. Allow these scriptures to fill your mind.

[1] Therefore, since we are surrounded by such a great cloud of witnesses, let us throw off everything that hinders and the sin that so easily entangles, and let us run with perseverance the race marked out for us. [2] Let us fix our eyes on Jesus, the author and perfecter of our faith,

who for the joy set before him endured the cross, scorning its shame, and sat down at the right hand of the throne of God. [3] *Consider him who endured such opposition from sinful men, so that you will not grow weary and lose heart.* [4] *In your struggle against sin, you have not yet resisted to the point of shedding your blood.* (Hebrews 12:1-4)

"Be careful," Jesus said to them. "Be on your guard against the yeast of the Pharisees and Sadducees." (Matthew 16:6)

Watch and pray so that you will not fall into temptation. The spirit is willing, but the body is weak. (Matthew 26:41)

Then [Jesus] said to them, "Watch out! Be on your guard against all kinds of greed; a man's life does not consist in the abundance of his possessions." (Luke 12:15)

Therefore, dear friends, since you already know this, be on your guard so that you may not be carried away by the error of lawless men and fall from your secure position. (2 Peter 3:17)

Here's putting things in perspective. As long as Eve was following the Lord, she was fine. But when the serpent deceived her, she ate (Genesis 3:13). Trickery always has been and always will be Satan's way of operating.

Our emotions become the very thing we lean on in times of trouble. We rely on our emotions and feelings, trusting more on our flesh than seeking God and His thoughts and ways. Isaiah 55:8 says, "For my thoughts are not your thoughts, neither are your ways my ways, declares the LORD." We think we can handle it, but our emotions are out of control.

Ever woke with Jesus on your mind? You prayed, wrote in your journal, sang a couple of hymns, went into a praise dance to find yourself throwing a tantrum an hour later. What happened? Allow me to be transparent once again. I recall a time when I spent time with the Lord and found myself in the best of mood. Life was good. Halfway through the morning, all hell broke loose. I am doing my best to keep my emotions intact, but soon found myself slamming my bedroom door yelling, "I'm sick of this!" My emotions were out of control. Glad no one was around to see my performance. Let's back up. I did mention that I spent time with the Lord and that life was good; right? So where did I go wrong? I allowed the frustration of everyday stuff and the insecurity of others to get the best of me. I often wonder if the enemy has some sort of radar that tells him, "Oh, she or he is feeling pretty good today. They think they have themselves together, so let's go and mess them up!" Truthfully, he is not that powerful. Yes, Satan is real, but there are many times we allow ourselves to walk into the traps and give in to our flesh.

The insecurity of others can bring about one emotionally or verbally abusing another. Valerie Bass, a LISW-S shares the following: "The main point about emotional and verbal abuse is that we control what we receive in our spirits and minds. We have a choice to believe what someone is speaking into our spirit. If someone is telling me that I am something other than what God says I am, I can choose not to receive their spoken word. Everyone makes mistakes, but our mistakes do not define us." Here's the challenge: a person with low self-esteem or a person who has a life of abuse will believe the lie. A person who has lived their life as a victim will believe the lies of the enemy. A person who has lived their life defeated will believe the lie.

Yes, abuse is serious. Women, men, and children throughout society are alive and well. In reading different publications, I think it is safe to say that insecure women talk a lot of trash and with the hopes of tearing the other person down without knowing they are working for the enemy. My husband once said, "People do what they do to others because they have not dealt with their own stuff." People may find themselves being abused emotionally and verbally because of the pain within another that has never been addressed. "Emotional and verbal abuse is anything that a person says or does to another person that causes them to be afraid, lowers a person's self esteem, or manipulates and controls another person's feelings or behavior. Examples: name calling and put downs; yelling and screaming; intentionally embarrassing a person in front of other people; telling an adult what to do; stalking; threatening suicide to manipulate another person; using internet or cell phones to control, intimidate, or humiliate." (www.thesafespace.org)

If you find yourself in an emotional or verbal abusive situation, please seek Christian counseling. Please do not allow this to become a stronghold of the enemy.

Let's pray:

Heavenly Father, we come to You through the precious blood of Jesus. Thank you, Lord, for protecting us. Thank You, Lord, for allowing Your ministering angels to encamp around us. Father, we ask You to destroy and remove any deception in our mind in the name of Jesus. Lord, in the name of Jesus we ask You to bind the power of Satan's demons and all dominion of darkness seeking a way to enter into our lives. Father, please bind all demonic assignments spoken or sent against us, and pronounce them to be no effect. "The reason the Son of God appeared was to destroy the devil's works" (1 John 3:8). Father, thank you for giving us strength to declare the ways and works of darkness that was placed over us is broken in the name of Jesus. Thank you Lord for binding the satanic forces of nature from harming Your children. We declare and decree that it is so in the name of Jesus. Amen.

DELIVERANCE, PLEASE!

I want to begin this chapter by asking a question. "Do you really want it?"

Let's look at John 5:1-9.

> ¹ *Some time later, Jesus went up to Jerusalem for a feast of the Jews.* ² *Now there is in Jerusalem near the Sheep Gate a pool, which in Aramaic is called Bethesda and which is surrounded by five covered colonnades.* ³ *Here a great number of disabled people used to lie – the blind, the lame, the paralyzed.* [4] [b] ⁵ *One who was there had been an invalid for thirty-eight years.* ⁶ *When Jesus saw him lying there and learned that he had been in this condition for a long time, he asked him, "Do you want to get well?"*
>
> ⁷ *"Sir," the invalid replied, "I have no one to help me into the pool when the water is stirred. While I am trying to get in, someone else goes down ahead of me."*
>
> ⁸ *Then Jesus said to him, "Get up! Pick up your mat and walk."* ⁹ *At once the man was cured; he picked up*

his mat and walked. The day on which this took place was a Sabbath.

You can receive your healing today—healing and deliverance from the lies that have been spoken into your life for so long. In the name of Jesus, I speak healing and deliverance. The choice is yours, and the question remains, "Do you really want it?"

Look at your life. Look at the lives of your loved ones and friends. Isn't it interesting when you look within your circle of relationships you see individuals who may be struggling and who are in bondage because of the life choices they have made. Many of those choices were made because of the lies that were once whispered into their spirits. Time and time again, individuals find themselves in unpleasant situations where they have become comfortable, only because they don't know anything different.

Perhaps you have heard this before or even said it yourself: "If I could only believe what God says about me and not keep living this way, I could get past this situation." IF has become the main attraction! "IF." "If" has become a part of your common vocabulary. No sooner do we get over one negative mindset only to walk into another, a potentially more difficult mindset that we'll need to overcome.

We want to be free. But, we become complacent in our mess. We understand all powers of darkness still have a deathly grip on our world. So we live with the terrible tension between what we experience and the life-speaking words of Jesus! Why can't we finally believe God?

In John 5:5, we see there was one who had been an invalid for thirty-eight years. This is refreshing for me. It tells me that no matter our age or how long we have been "disabled," we can be delivered from the lies that the enemy has told us. No matter what state we are in, Jesus sees all and will come to intervene and set us free. John 5:6 reads that "When Jesus saw him lying there and learned he had been in this condition for a long time, he asked him, "Do you want to get well?" I believe that Jesus is asking each of us "Do you want to be delivered from the lies of the enemy?

As we read further in the text, this man points out that he has no one to help him get to the pool. Our similar response would sound much like this: "While I'm trying to get my life in order, something else always happens" or "I'm trying to get over this thing, but then I can't do that because of ..." It is time that we make up in our minds that we truly want to be set free, walk into the truth and expose the enemy's lies. We must choose to answer Jesus' question. The lame man initially focused on why he had not gotten well and how he had been mistreated or left alone.

Here are a couple of questions for us. Why do we so often depend on others to help us? Why are we so afraid to step out on our own to change our course?

I don't know about you, but after being in this situation for thirty-eight years, I hope that I would have said YES without hesitation. But that's not what happens here. What this man says in response amazes me. This man does not answer Jesus' question, but says "Sir, I have no one to put me into the pool when the water is stirred; and while I am making my way, someone else steps down ahead of me." Now, isn't that just like you and me? We have issues and challenges and are in need of healing and deliverance and are all waiting, wanting to be healed. Instead of answering Jesus, we choose to make excuses and continue the life we have, choosing to remain in bondage.

Unfortunately, sometimes individuals have been in their situation for so long that they choose to stay "comfortable" in what should be an uncomfortable place. This is all they know; therefore, they make the choice to stay in the familiar. They have lived the lie for so long that there is no reason to change it now. I believe a lot of this has to do with fear. People profess to want help—help to get out of their life of lies, but are afraid of what may come with the change. They are afraid of a new life, a life free of bondage and lies.

I will ask again. Do you really want it? Are you ready to be delivered from the enemy's lies about your life and who you are?

At some point, you will have to take the initiative. Start using your voice for your freedom. This man during his conversation with Jesus showed no hope. He had no hope of ever being delivered and no desire to help himself. This man merely offers an excuse.

We are notoriously resistant to change, even when change can bring us out of bondage. We have ways of extracting "secondary gain" from our infirmities, and we do not easily let go of the chains that hold us bound. For thirty-eight years he had learned to be comfortable in his sickness. Here it is: We get addicted to our weakness and disabilities. Our discomfort becomes comfortable once everything in our life is ordered around it. It's easier for us to see how we cannot be healed. It's easier for us to make excuses and doubt.

We seem to build walls of excuses around our situations so we don't have to face them. We know that God is speaking to us, but we manage to ignore Him. It is easier for us to listen to and believe the lies of the enemy. We ask the Lord to heal us, but we continue in our sickness because we're used to it, and it's easier to stay in it than to get out of it. Every weakness, sickness, discouragement, etc. is caused by our unwillingness to do what it takes to be free from the lies that so easily beset us. We cannot let a problem or hardship cause us to lose hope. Many of us are living our lives just as the lame man.

It is time to expect an unanticipated act of grace from our Lord and Savior Jesus Christ. Let's continue going through this scripture and look at verse 8. Jesus doesn't give any attention to the man's nonsense about how no one was helping him and so on. Jesus just said, "Get up! Pick up your mat and walk." While this man is talking in circles, never answering Jesus' question, Jesus cuts through and speaks an authoritative word. Jesus speaks life! The Bible says in Proverbs 18:21, "The tongue has the power of life and death, and those who love it will eat its fruit." Which fruit will you enjoy?

Today, you have a decision to make. You can receive your deliverance from the lies the enemy has told you or you may choose to stay in the same place you've been. Today, you can begin a new life, one that includes the power of God over your weakness, your sickness, your low self-esteem, and your sin. You can choose this day to pick up your mat and walk in freedom — the freedom from the lies that have kept you bound.

It's enough with the excuses. It's enough with the reasons why you cannot overcome the lies that have held you captive. It is up to you to believe God and to live into truth. Again, I ask, do you want to be delivered from the lies of the enemy? Do you really want it?

I dare you to be free from the lies of the enemy! I double dare you! It's up to you. You can choose to stay where you are, or you can believe God and receive your deliverance today.

Who Told You That you had to be bound to the lies of the enemy? *Who Told You That?*

And now you know...

I'm Coming Out!

Your introduction began the day your mother pushed you through the birthing canal and the doctor said, "It's a girl" or "It's a boy."

Come along with me and travel down the highway of imagination. Imagine, if you will, that you have been recommended by a committee of an elite society to be a debutante and be presented during the Cotillion, which is a formal affair. As you wait to be presented by your escort into society wearing your long white gown, crinoline, long satin gloves, you take your walk to curtsy, receive your bouquet of roses; you are then received by your handsome date. If you are a gentleman, you are dressed in your tux with your bow-tie, white gloves, and shiny black shoes. Whether you are the male or the female being presented to society, you stand in the receiving line to begin the waltz, which is the mark of a new day.

Imagine that you are about to graduate, which comes with senior pictures, cap and gown measurements, the prom, senior night, senior trip, invitations, waiting on your moment to hear your name announced, you cross the stage, receive your diploma, only to turn your tassel to step into a new era of life.

Imagine as a female you have been asked by your prince to take his hand in marriage. The wedding day has arrived and all eyes are on you as you take your walk down the aisle. You are flanked by bridesmaids, maid and matron of honor, and a flower girl dropping rose petals down the aisle. You make a covenant before the Lord and say, "I do" to start your journey when the preacher says, "Now I pronounce you man and wife!" There's clapping, cheers, and well wishes.

As you read Luke 8:40-48 you will notice that **This is NOT this woman's story!** And for many of us—it's not our story EITHER! This woman could have only wished to be presented in this fashion of a cotillion, a graduation, a large wedding. She would have loved to have had the opportunity to have a coming out celebration to the world and be accepted. She would have loved to have felt special: A party, and for the world to know that she has arrived. But, like many women in the world today, they make a statement after hearing about such events and say, "I know this couldn't happen for me!"

How long shall one hide behind the mask that represents lies? How long shall one seek the advice of others? How much money shall one spend to get answers that can only be found in the book of life? At what point do we take the risk and completely walk by faith? When shall we expose ourselves and tell Jesus our entire story?

Let us look at Luke 8:40-48 which says,

> [40] *Now when Jesus returned, a crowd welcomed him, for they were all expecting him.* [41] *Then a man named Jairus, a ruler of the synagogue, came and fell at Jesus' feet, pleading with him to come to his house* [42] *because his only daughter, a girl of about twelve, was dying.*
>
> *As Jesus was on his way, the crowds almost crushed him.* [43] *And a woman was there who had been subject to bleeding for twelve years, but no one could heal her.* [44] *She came up behind him and touched the edge of his cloak, and immediately her bleeding stopped.*
>
> [45] *"Who touched me?" Jesus asked.*
>
> *When they all denied it, Peter said, "Master, the people are crowding and pressing against you."*
>
> [46] *But Jesus said, "Someone touched me; I know that power has gone out from me."*
>
> [47] *Then the woman, seeing that she could not go unnoticed, came trembling and fell at his feet. In the presence of all the people, she told why she had touched him and how she had been instantly healed.* [48] *Then he said to her, "Daughter, your faith has healed you. Go in peace."*

This woman was in this position for twelve years. She experienced this issue of bleeding and searched for answers from others, but no one could heal her. After she heard that Jesus would be in the area, she made a decision to risk everything by being in the community as an unclean woman. Her life would be in danger. There were rules; however, she made the decision to break the rule in order to do what she could to touch the hem of Jesus' garment. She did it. She took a risk, came out into society and made her way to Jesus. One could only imagine that she was on her stomach inching her way through the crowd. Was she being stepped on? Was she being kicked? Wonder what it was like for her to be down low to the ground, hoping and praying to touch the very hem of Jesus. She touched Him. Yes, she did. And immediately she was healed. Can you imagine an immediate healing because you decided to risk it all to get to Christ?

Upon hearing Jesus was coming to town this woman had to have a plan. Yes? Did she have her course of action mapped out? I can hear her now asking, "How do I get to Him? What will be my strategy? What route will I take? How can I sneak in, touch Him and go? What shall I wear? How shall I act?"

The Bible continues the story by saying, "As Jesus was on his way, the crowds almost crushed him. And a woman was there who had been subject to bleeding for twelve years, but no one could heal her." People who will read this book may think "No one can heal me." May I suggest that we take on the form of this woman? This woman did not care at that moment what would happen to her, she just moved forward in her faith. She heard about a man named Jesus who was coming to town. She made the decision not to hide any longer. She was considered unclean and had no business being out in the community. But she did what she needed to do to get to the Master Himself!

Throw yourself all in and make it happen. Verse 44 of the Scripture in Luke 8 says, "She came up behind him and touched the edge of his cloak..." This is when you make the decision to know and understand that the Lord loves you. This is when you make the decision not to be ashamed. This is when you are no longer shy or conservative. This is when you are no longer ashamed of your choices you've made in the past. This is when you know that you now make better choices because you are following Christ. When you make the decision to throw yourself all in! There's nothing holding you back, therefore, do not hold anything back. Give it what you got! No turning back! You've come too far! You're either in or you're not! Make the choice to say, "YES!" And then you're there!!! Go ahead, reach out and TOUCH HIM!!! Your healing is within reach. It really does not matter what happens next. The only thing that matters is that you are following through with the faith you have built up—although it may be small as a mustard seed—it's enough! Go for it!

Realize that you have the best director. The Lord orchestrated the opportunity for this woman to be reintroduced to society. So much so, that she received a standing ovation. As she was crawling on her hands, knees, and belly, the people all around her were standing and shouting. What a crowd. Jesus drew attention to the woman by asking, "Who touched me?" Which gave the "Spotlight" to the woman as she made her debut.

Verse 45 asks the question, "Who touched me?"

All eyes were on the one who touched Jesus! Everyone is looking around waiting to see just who touched the Savior! What awe! What a surprise! What? Who? Why? Where is this person? We want to see who was BOLD enough to touch the Master!

Please do not be fooled! There will always be someone in the crowd trying to take your spotlight! Peter had to open his mouth and say, "Master, the people are crowding and pressing against you." Peter didn't know His daughter had arrived!

But Jesus said, "Someone touched me; I know that power has gone out from me."

"The woman, seeing that she could not go unnoticed, came trembling and fell at his feet. In the presence of all the people, she told why she had touched him..." (verse 47).

Her story went something like this: I have been bleeding for twelve years, I have seen many doctors, I didn't have faith, I didn't trust you, I didn't believe in you, I didn't think you loved me, I didn't... (you fill in the blank).

Your story may flow like this: I had a man in my life, but he treated me bad. I had a wife who made the decision to walk out on me and our relationship. I had premature children. I have a child who was diagnosed with cancer. Can I prove myself worthy to God? Can the Lord really bring me through the fire? Will I be able to see the reflection of God when I look in the mirror?

How wonderful to hear Jesus say, "Your faith has healed you!" Even within the crowd, Jesus knew who touched Him. As Jesus is having this conversation with the woman, whom He later called daughter, the people were standing around. What a debut! You cannot ask for anything better than that. Can you see it? You are going through life struggles. Life has you in a chokehold, but Jesus places a label on you such as son or daughter. Up until this point of your life, you have kept your head down. You seldom come out into the community. You know because of your issues that everyone who knows about you has talked about you. You believed the lies that your life will never get any better, but just then, you hear about Jesus and decide to take a risk and come out of your past. Right now, as you are reading this chapter in this book you can be healed in the name of Jesus. Whatever you are doing, ask the Lord to heal you. Make it up in your mind to come out of your past and step by faith into your now and your tomorrow. It's yours.

This woman was being presented to the world by God. Each person standing around would witness a woman fully aware and extremely grateful for the immeasurable amount of grace she has been given. Sometimes overwhelmed by the blessing and gifts that He has bestowed on her, He would not have to remind her of all that He has charged her to do and accomplish. This is not outside of our reach. God knows the plans He has for us (Jeremiah 29:11).

With head held high and shoulders back, walk in the grace and mercy He has given unto you. It's time for you to come out. Come out from behind the masks and the lies that have dressed you for so many years. God has placed this book in your hands for such a time as this. He has some amazing things for you to do.

Thinking back to your past you recall the lies, but now ask yourself, "Who Told Me That?" The enemy who has tried to keep you bound. Today you are free in the name of Jesus.

And now you know...

TrUTh

HOLY DISGUISED

We all should know the hymn, "Holy, Holy, Holy" which was written by Reginald Heber in 1862. He wrote the hymn for Trinity Sunday while he was Vicar of Hodnet, Shropshire, England. The hymn taken from Isaiah 6:3 with the lyrics:

Holy, holy, holy! Lord God Almighty!
Early in the morning, our song shall rise to thee.
Holy, holy, holy! Merciful and mighty,
God in three persons blessed Trinity!

Holy, holy, holy! All the saints adore thee,
casting down their golden crowns around the
    glassy sea;
cherubim and seraphim falling down before thee,
which wert, and art, and evermore shalt be?

Holy, holy, holy! Though the darkness hide thee,
Though the eye of sinful man thy glory may
   not see,
Only thou art holy; there is none beside thee,
Perfect in power, in love and purity.

Holy, holy, holy! Lord God Almighty!
All thy works shall praise thy name, in earth
   and sky and sea.
Holy, holy, holy! Merciful and mighty,
God in three persons blessed Trinity.

What a wonderful hymn to plant deep in your spirit and soul. Holy, Holy, Holy! Lord God Almighty! He is mighty. He is wonderful. He is merciful. He is most holy. All shall praise His name. God is Father, Son, and Holy Spirit. Why then do we lie on Him? Wasn't expecting that question were you?

It is amazing how often people will lie on the Holy Spirit. In speaking with a pastor friend, we shared how interesting it is that people will approach another and say, "The Holy Spirit told me to tell you (blank)." First thought, "Who Told You That?" obviously it's not Christ because He would have at least mentioned it to me. There would be some sort of witness to my spirit. Often no one corrects the person who has said something that does not bear witness with your spirit, therefore, we allow individuals to lie on Jesus. I am not sure if we are afraid that we will hurt someone's feeling or interfere with their walk with God or if we are afraid that they will view us as one without Christ. Whatever the reason, one must be careful in saying such, especially if it's not true. And if it is not true, you have just lied on the Holy Spirit. Lying on God is dangerous.

Let's talk about this. Why is there a need to tell a lie on God? The Bible says in Isaiah 6, "God is holy." Ministering over the last several years, there seems to be a need for people to feel as if they have a direct connection with Jesus. Here's the truth, you don't need to prove anything. Let your walk with the Lord speak for itself. However, for so many that is not enough. So people portray themselves as super holy. When someone brings you a word from the Lord it should be a word of confirmation, not something you have never heard before.

We also read in James 5:19-20 in the New Living Translation, "My dear brothers and sisters, if someone among you wanders away from the truth and is brought back, you can be sure that whoever brings the sinner back will save that person from death and bring about the forgiveness of many sins." This translates to say, if there is someone in our life who has left the truth we should do our best to bring them back to the truth for we will save that person from death; that is spiritual death.

Another Scripture one could refer to is found in, Ephesians 4:17-18, which reads, "With the Lord's authority I say this: Live no longer as the Gentiles do, for they are hopelessly confused. Their minds are full of darkness; they wander far from the life God gives because they have closed their minds and hardened their hearts against him" (NLT). People become confused. They try hard to live a life holy and acceptable unto God, but try to walk out their belief under their own guidance. People are popping up everywhere calling themselves, prophets, apostles, and prophetesses, speaking lies instead of the truth. I cannot say it's done on purpose. It appears that people are really trying to live a life of Christ, but get caught up in wanting people to believe they have a direct connect more so than you. Allow me to be clear; there are true prophets, apostles, and prophetesses called by God, and they are doing so under His leading where He is receiving all the glory and the honor. Jesus is the one being high and lifted up.

This is what is bothersome. The Old Testament talks about the priest going to God on our behalf, but the New Testament tells us that the curtain was torn and we now have direct access. So, if that is true, and it is, we can speak to Jesus directly. When that is suggested, people become offended. Look at Leviticus 19:12: "Do not swear falsely by my name and so profane the name of your God. I am the LORD."

Proverbs 26:28 says, "A lying tongue hates those it hurts, and a flattering mouth works ruin." How many people have you hurt because you lied on the Holy Spirit by saying, "The Holy Spirit said (blank)"? We wonder why people leave the church, leave the faith, stop trusting in Jesus. At some point we must return to lifting the name of Jesus for His name is to be high and lifted up. He is the great I Am. He is God. He is holy! He is King and Lord. And yes, He is Savior! There are people who are afraid of people. No, it's time to be afraid of lying on the Holy One who is Jesus Christ our Lord and Savior.

Allow me to give some cutting truth. The Bible says in Hebrews 4: 12-13, "For the word of God is living and active. Sharper than any double-edged sword, it penetrates even to dividing soul and spirit, joints and marrow; it judges the thoughts and attitudes of the heart. Nothing in all creation is hidden from God's sight. Everything is uncovered and lay bare before the eyes of him to whom we must give account." Meaning the word is alive, and it is always working. The Word of God is truth, and it is active. It will cut while judging thoughts and attitudes. Absolutely nothing can hide from God. Every word spoken by you will be revealed, and at some point you will have to give an account. If you are questioning what is considered a lie allow me to be clear.

- The completion of a half-truth sentence — is a lie.
- When a sentence is used to mislead or deceive someone else — it is a lie.
- Half a truth is a whole lie.
- .0000001 % of a lie makes the remaining percentage that is true — a lie.

God is Holy. He is a God that will not lie. (Numbers 23:19)

So again, one must ask, "Who Told You That?"
And now you know…

The Truth About the Lies

So many lies and so much bondage! Where do we turn from here? There's so much to uncover that we can't possibly discuss it all in one book. These untruths have been a part of our life for so long that realistically, the process will take some time. The serpent did his best to destroy Eve. There are some people who cross our path who will do their best to keep us in bondage, and some will even try to destroy us. Praise God for His truth that says, "For I know the plans I have for you," says the LORD. "They are plans for good and not for disaster, to give you a future and a hope. In those days when you pray, I will listen" (Jeremiah 29:11-12, NLT).

In the chapter, "Please Do Not Try to Silence Me," I asked the question about women being silent in the church. Does this continue today where women feel like they have no voice in the church?

A friend of mine, Trina Pockett, asked this question on her blog at TrinaPockett.com: Should women be silent in church? Trina directed us to 1 Corinthians 14:34-35.

"Women should be silent during the church meetings. It is not proper for them to speak. They should be submissive, just as the law says. If they have any questions, they should ask their husbands at home, for it is improper for women to speak in church meetings." Trina says, "This portion of scripture has been used for years to keep women quiet in the church. Women have been delegated to 'women's roles' in the church, women's ministry, the nursery and the kitchen. Women need to have a voice. We make up half the church."

As a woman, a wife, a Christian, a pastor, and a mom to a teenage daughter, I felt a need to weigh in on the subject. I have been taught to always read before and after the selected scripture. After reading 1 Corinthians 14, I conclude that yes, women do have a voice. Verse 30 states, "And if a revelation comes to someone who is sitting down, the first speaker should stop." God gives revelation to whomever He chooses to give it to. Therefore, if He gives this revelation to a woman and it is for the body, she has a responsibility to the body. Then, in verse 31, "For you can all prophesy in turn so that everyone may be instructed and encouraged." Notice it says "all." This scripture does not single out any particular gender. The proper context is that there was division in that particular church during that time. This scripture does not refer to every church and every situation.

So, what would happen if the woman is without a husband? Can an unmarried woman not speak? I recall Paul saying, "Now to the unmarried and the widows I say: It is good for them to stay unmarried, as I do" (1 Corinthians 7:8). So, if it's good to stay unmarried for the individuals who are able to control themselves from sexual desires as scripture states, there would be no husband to confer with before the meeting. Right? There are great women preachers and teachers who God has called to change the world through their spoken message. Silence? No. Obedience? Yes.

By reading this scripture without context, we may believe that women should be silent in church. To some degree, people may believe women should be silent at home and throughout the community. However, this is not what this scripture is saying.

Let's look at the church and some of the lies that are told. Let's see what causes some of the confusion. In the survey, I asked individuals about their experiences at church and the church rules they witnessed. Here is a random sample of what was shared.

- "Only the elect and wives of pastors are allowed to sit on the front pews of the church."
- "Pastor's wives are to sit in the second pew."
- "Pants are not allowed in the church sanctuary."
- "God is offended if I did not dress up for church."
- "When I join church, my life will be great."
- "The pastor and his/her spouse will become my friends."

- "Everyone truly loves and likes each other in the church."
- "People who speak in tongues are weird and crazy. But if you don't speak in tongues, you are not saved."
- If you had a baby and you were not married, you had to go before the church and confess."
- "During your teenage years, when someone called a girl a "Jezebel" it meant she was fast or a whore."
- "As long as you repent, everything will be ok and there won't be any consequences."
- "If you committed suicide, you were going to hell."
- "Praise and worship is real only when you get the Holy Ghost and shout. But you have to "catch" the Holy Ghost."
- "Church is not church unless people shouted and spoke in tongues."
- "Real church is held on Sunday at 11am in a church building."

The Word tells us to "study to shew thyself approved unto God, a workman that needeth not to be ashamed, rightly dividing the word of truth" (2 Timothy 2:15, KJV). I am going to make a bold statement: People are lazy. We would rather have someone tell us what is in the Bible than actually read it ourselves. My husband is a senior pastor and a seminary professor. However, I take the scriptures he preaches in his sermon or teaches in Bible study and I review and meditate to seek revelation knowledge for myself. There are times when I will challenge something he says because my interpretation is completely different from his.

In the list of quotes that were shared by the survey respondents, we see that many of the "rules" and ideas of church were made by man and not according to the Bible. These beliefs are made up. For example, "Real church is held on Sunday's at 11 a.m. in a church building." Who told you that? The Bible I read says, "For where two or three gather in my name, there am I with them" (Matthew 18:20). This scripture does not tell us in what type of place or what time church service must be held.

Once, I attended a church where there was a sign over the sanctuary door that read, "No Pants Allowed." I laughed to myself and said, "Well, I guess every man waiting to go to church today won't be able to go in!" When we read the Bible, what do we read? What are the people wearing? Were men in slacks? Let's look at the response, "God is offended if I am not dressed up." What about individuals who cannot afford suits and dresses that are "church-appropriate"? What about the homeless? Nowhere in the Bible does it say that you are to dress a specific way to come to church. What is important to God is that we have a personal relationship with Him. It is important to God that we spend time with Him. He really doesn't care what we have on our bodies. It's what is in our hearts that matters.

Another quote I would like to address is the one that reads, "Pastors' wives are to sit on the second pew of the church." That's interesting. First of all, I don't find this in the Bible, and secondly, in biblical times, women were to be in the back of the temple. So exactly where did we get this notion that the wives of pastors are to sit in the second pew? Who told you that? It's made up. These are the rules we make up to keep everyone in a particular box. It's time to rip the box apart and live according to the Word of the Lord. The woman in Luke 13 who was bent for eighteen years was clearly sitting in the back of the synagogue. How do we know? If we read the scriptures, we will see that the Lord called her forward. If she was up front, He would have simply touched her where He stood. So, could it be that today pastors' wives may sit wherever they choose?

Another interesting quote is, "The pastor and his or her spouse will become my friends." The enemy really tries to trip us up with this one. This is one of the lies that can cause division in a church. Pastors (male or female) have a life of their own. They are able to choose who they call friend. It is not about the church membership. As soon as something appears not to work out in our favor, we blame the pastor and the spouse. We are now angry and will leave the church. We feel a special "privilege" and when the pastor and his or her spouse don't follow our direction or command, we're frustrated. The pastor and his or her spouse cannot be everything for everyone. It is unrealistic. The enemy wants you to follow your pastor, a man or a woman, not God. Develop your relationship with Jesus and do not put all of your trust in the pastor, his or her family, and the church. They will disappoint you. Not intentionally, but realistically, it will happen.

We are very good at blaming God. "It's all God's fault," we say when something goes wrong in our life and in the life of the church. No, it is not. God gives us free will. So often we abuse our freedom. Actually, the moment we give our life to Christ, the enemy steps up his game because he has lost another soul from his camp. He is not going to allow us to move along as if all is well. He is seeking whom he may devour. Ephesians 6 says,

> [10] *Finally, be strong in the Lord and in his mighty power.* [11] *Put on the full armor of God, so that you can take your stand against the devil's schemes.* [12] *For our struggle is not against flesh and blood, but against the rulers, against the authorities, against the powers of this dark world and against the spiritual forces of evil in the heavenly realms.* [13] *Therefore, put on the full armor of God, so that when the day of evil comes, you may be able to stand your ground, and after you have done everything, to stand.* [14] *Stand firm then, with the belt of truth buckled around your waist, with the breastplate of righteousness in place,* [15] *and with your feet fitted with the readiness that comes from the gospel of peace.* [16] *In addition to all this, take up the shield of faith, with which you can extinguish all the flaming arrows of the*

evil one. [17] Take the helmet of salvation and the sword of the Spirit, which is the word of God.

[18] And pray in the Spirit on all occasions with all kinds of prayers and requests. With this in mind, be alert and always keep on praying for all the Lord's people. [19] Pray also for me, that whenever I speak, words may be given me so that I will fearlessly make known the mystery of the gospel, [20] for which I am an ambassador in chains. Pray that I may declare it fearlessly, as I should. (Ephesians 6:10-20)

Let's break this down. First, we have to be strong in the Lord, followed by putting on the full armor of God. Here's a funny. I was taught that each morning, I needed to get up and physically put on the armor of God, as if I was getting dressed! I have learned over the years that it is not that deep. It is about reading God's Word, fasting and praying. It was not about putting on clothing. Quite frankly, as I write this, I realize that I was caught up in something that someone told me to do and never thought to ask why. The scripture continues saying that in putting on the full armor of God, we will be able to stand against the devil's schemes. "For our struggle is not against flesh and blood, but against the rulers, against the authorities, against the powers of this dark world and against the spiritual forces of evil in the heavenly realms." The truth is that we cannot fight the devil in our own strength. Only

God can. It's a lie to believe you can fight the devil in your own strength and win.

Let's look at one more of the responses to the survey. "When I join church, my life will be great." My first thought is, "Really?" So often people believe that if you join up with God, all the struggles magically go away. The concept of "joining a church" rubs me the wrong way. Here's the truth. We are joining the Body of Christ, which means you can attend any church you are led to attend. However, some pastors believe they have a "contract" with certain people in their churches, not allowing those people to leave the church. Please allow me the chance to explain. When you accept Christ as your personal savior, you join the Body of Christ. When you become a member or a partner of a particular church, you are aligning yourself with that fellowship. You should find a church which is Bible-based and secondly, a place where you can learn and grow. However, you are responsible for your personal growth, meaning that you are to further your development through ongoing Bible study, time of fellowship with Jesus, and participating in the fellowship you have been led to align yourself with.

As Christians, we become frustrated and confuse the truth with lies. We have the audacity to make church and church life about ourselves. The song "It's Not About Us" by Bishop Noel Jones and The City of Refuge Choir, says clearly that it is about Jesus, not about us. We want Jesus to fit our lifestyle, our agenda, our comfort, and our convenience. It is as if we have a menu of services we want and desire, and if Christianity or church life does not match what we are looking for, we go elsewhere. The truth is that there is neither a church nor a fellowship that will match all of what you are looking for. Here is another truth: every church or fellowship will bring you discipline at one point or another. There is no perfect church. David Platt says he "...could not help but think about somewhere along the way we had missed what is radical about our faith and replaced it with what is comfortable. ... (there is a) settling for a Christianity that revolves around catering to ourselves when the central message of Christianity is actually about abandoning ourselves." It is time to abandon ourselves and live in the truth of Jesus.

There are so many church-related "rules and regulations." As you reflect on your own experiences in the church, consider where these "traditions" came from. Are they biblical? Or are they made up? Many of the things we believe and the traditions we continue in the church are all lies. Personally, I have been told lie after lie when it comes to the church and church relations. I can do this, but I can't do that. Who told you that?

Returning to the survey, here are some additional responses dealing with how respondents feel about themselves based on what they have been told.

- "I believed I was dirty, unlovable, and different from everyone else because I was sexually molested as a three-year-old. I actually believed it was somehow my fault and the shame was with me my whole life like a weight around my neck. The person who did this finally admitted it fifty years later. He thought I didn't remember it, but I did. I know Satan kept me in bondage to the lies."

- "I look in the mirror and see someone unattractive."
- "I am not worth anything because I cannot afford the greater things of life."
- "I am not worthy of anything good."
- "I will never get married."
- "I will never be healed."
- "I will never have anything to share with others."
- "I will never complete school."
- "I was told that my skin is too dark and no one wants to be with a dark-skinned person."
- "I'm too white."
- "I'm stupid."
- "I will never accomplish much."

Lie after lie after lie. It's time to stop believing the lies. We put so much focus on ourselves. I can go through the Bible and give truth back to negate each lie. Lot's wife didn't believe and she looked back. We know what happened to her. Orpah wanted to return home to what she believed was a place filled with milk and honey. Once she turned back, we never heard of her again. Ruth, on the other hand, lived a pretty good life. Naomi was perceived as bitter, but when you continue reading about her in the Book of Ruth, she became a leader.

I was told that having a son out of wedlock would cause my son to become nothing and that I would never be able to find a good husband. My son is a college graduate and a youth pastor, and is doing very well for himself. I have one dynamite husband who walks with the Lord, has a Doctor of Ministry and is completing a PhD. Just think if I would have listened to the lies! What if I had given up my son for adoption because I thought I wasn't "suitable"? What if I never risked love with anyone? Someone else would have cared for my son and some other woman would be enjoying the husband that was ordained for me. Brother, sister, you need to ask yourself the question: Who told you that?

It's time to look in the mirror and say, "I look good." "I am wonderfully and uniquely made" (Psalm 139).

It is time to take the necessary steps to complete school, start your business, or take a chance on yourself to reach your dreams. Stop making excuses. Stop saying you can't afford it or you don't have the resources to make it happen. There are resources, people, grants, and scholarships that will sow seeds into your education and your dreams. Just do it!

It is time to believe God and stop believing the enemy's lies. The enemy began lying early as soon as humans came on the scene. He arrived in the Garden and tempted the woman, setting the stage for the fall. Every day we fall for something. But we don't have to.

Here's some final truth. We blame so much on the enemy. The enemy could be within you and me. It is easy to blame others. However, we set ourselves up to fall. Romans 12 points out that we are to renew our minds daily.

Use the following journal to record the lies that have been spoken into your spirit. Be honest. Be clear. Be descriptive. Make the decision to begin today and live in the truth of what Jesus says. Remember, "In the beginning, God" (Genesis 1). Throughout the entire first chapter, God said, "It is good." That statement alone is really all we need. "It is good!"

We would love to hear from you. Please visit us at our blog, http://atthetablewithgail.blogspot.com, and share in the discussions. Monthly we post a blog asking the question, "Who Told You That?" feel free to join the conversation. It is time to break free from the traps of deception and change the lies into the truth God has for you.

THE BATTLE BELONGS TO GOD

Every day, we are faced with potentially challenging life situations. Oftentimes, we find ourselves on the frontline or at least in the middle of a battle and possibly up against insurmountable odds. We take a look at our lives and find that our finances have hit rock bottom, causing us great stress and worry. Our bills could be out of control, the rent or mortgage is due and, for some, months behind. Children may be acting as if they have lost their minds and behaving completely out of character. On top of all that, our job situation is on shaky ground, and if we're married, the relationship may be giving you a fit. To put the cherry on top, you are ready to lose all self-control, and your health is deteriorating, all because of the stress of fighting this battle that doesn't even belong to you.

We tend to see things in the negative because we have allowed Satan to gain ground in our lives. He has whispered the untruths long enough and now it is time to give this battle over to the Lord.

You may be in a situation right now where you have no idea what is about to happen and how things will actually work out. You cannot sleep at night and you walk the floors trying to figure this thing out all by yourself. Here's a secret: this battle belongs to the Lord! You may find yourself rocking back and forth not knowing what to do, or calling anyone and everyone you know hoping someone can figure it out for you only to find out that rocking doesn't work and nobody can give you the answer, even if they care enough to try. Your spirit isn't settled. You have an ongoing headache and your blood pressure is rising. It doesn't matter what the situation is. You may be in the middle of a legal battle, a battle for your health, a financial battle or a relationship battle. Whatever the battle is, remember that it is not yours, it is the Lord's. Therefore, let it go. No longer give the enemy a foothold by staying in it. Give it to God.

In everyday life, we deal with obstacles. Some obstacles are larger than others, but we must stand our ground. In 2 Chronicles 20:17, it states that *"You will not have to fight this battle. Take up your positions; stand firm and see the deliverance the* LORD *will give you."* "Take up your position" means to make a decision and stand on the decision you have made. Your position should be a position of confidence. Confidence that the Lord our God already knows what you are going through and that He will take care of you as you go through it. Stand, knowing that no matter what the outcome is, that "God knows the plans He has for you. Plans to give you a future and a hope; not plans for destruction" (Jeremiah 29:11). If God already knows the course of your future and if you trust Him, you can just stand. It's already stated that "you will not have to fight this battle." Why is it then that we don't believe it? Why do we still continue to fight on our own? Is it that we try to fight the battle so we can feel better?

I challenge this thought process. I don't believe that we actually feel better because we are fighting the battle. The reason I challenge this is because so often I have found myself trying to fight whichever battle it is at the time realizing later that I did not fully trust God. As I was trying to win the battle, all the while losing it, I found myself worn out, tired and worse off than when I began fighting. Turning our situations over to God is the answer. He has already said, "You will not have to fight this battle." There comes a point where we need to realize that the only answer is to believe God.

It is great news to know that we can believe God. This is freeing! Believing God frees us to let go! It forces us and allows us to focus on standing firm, on trusting and believing what God says. It is easy to take our ball and run home so that we can throw our own pity party. It is easy to eat everything in sight, cry ourselves to sleep, and call all of our friends for advice, looking for sympathy and agreement. Yes, those things are easy, but with God, the outcome will be His will and everything will be under His authority and His control. Sit still; this is not your battle. We have to get to the point where we really rest in His arms and trust Him. At some point, we must let go and fully serve God in spirit and in truth, and to be obedient to His will and His calling on our lives. If we would fully surrender to Christ, He will give us the words to speak and the actions to take when we are faced with a trial before us. He will give us the grace to extend when our flesh wants to show something of our natural state. Let's keep it real. It is not always that we want to share the love and offer grace. There are many times when we simply want our flesh to respond in immediate action. But God is calling us to simply "get in position," a position that allows Him to fight this battle. This battle is not ours, but it is the Lord's.

There are many battles in the world around us, but we must also remember the words in 2 Chronicles 20:15:

He said: "Listen, King Jehoshaphat and all who live in Judah and Jerusalem! This is what the Lord says to you: 'Do not be afraid or discouraged because of this vast army. For the battle is not yours, but God's.'"

Sad to say, but many of God's children walk around afraid and discouraged. That is why He said, "Do not be afraid or discouraged." God knew that would be our first position, the position of fear. In the name of Jesus, be delivered from fear! I love this phrase from Joyce Meyer: "Fear stands for False Evidence Appearing Real." Let's go a step further and say that fear is just an illusion. It is not real so there is no reason for you to be afraid. Here is an example of what we do: We get behind on some bills, we avoid answering the phone, thinking that the collector on the other end could do something more painful to us. First of all, the bill is due and if a collector is calling, it is delinquent. Not answering the phone is only going to make the situation worse. Not answering the phone to talk with the collector will weigh heavier on you in the end because nothing is being done about the delinquent bill and then there is the added guilt about avoiding the phone calls. Answer the telephone and speak with the person. Make some sort of arrangement and follow through. Being honest about our situations can lead to blessings from God in the process of settling your bill. There is nothing to fear. "You won't have to fight," you can just answer the phone! Stop allowing Satan to whisper in your ear that if you don't answer it, things will be alright. That's a lie!

We have much work before us in building the Kingdom. It starts with both you and me. God is calling us to get in position. He's telling us, "Don't be afraid or be discouraged." He then calls us forward by saying, "Go out and face them." Nothing more and nothing less. Be strong in the Lord. Be of good courage. Yes, tough times are before us, but nothing is greater than the God we serve.

Who Told You That the battle was yours? *Who Told You That?* The battle is not yours, it's the Lord's.

And now you know…

SURELY
YOU WON'T DIE

Truth:

It is possible you will die spiritually if you decide to
continue to believe the lies.

KNOW THE TRUTH
STUDY GOD'S WORD

[16] *"All Scripture is God-breathed and is useful for teaching, rebuking, correcting and training in righteousness,* [17] *so that the man of God may be thoroughly equipped for every good work."* 2 Timothy 3:16-17

Inductive Study Method

This is only one Bible Study method. The "Inductive study method" draws you into personal interaction with the Scriptures which consists of three components.

- Observation
- Interpretation
- Application

By utilizing this method of study, you will discover God's truth yourself, without leaning on the opinions and commentary of others. This personal discovery develops your confidence in understanding God's message of truth and love personally to you.

Inductive Bible study begins by carefully examining the biblical text. The first step, observation:

Observation answers the question: "What does the passage of scripture say?" This is the foundation which must be laid first if you want to accurately interpret and have right application for God's Word. It is discovering what is being said — and this requires time and practice.

Taking time to observe scriptures leads to correct interpretation and provides the foundation for personal application. Always begin with prayer for the Lord to open your eyes and illumine His truth in your heart and mind through His Spirit. God provides each believer with a personal teacher in the person of the Holy Spirit, Who enlightens our minds.

First: Pray

Second: Evaluate the content

    A) Observe: What do you see?
- Who is in the passage? (what is their involvement?)
- What are they saying?
- Where is this taking place?

- When is it happening? (timeframe, what's the history, etc.)
- Why? (facts, information, clues)

B) Interpret: What does it mean?
  - Why is he writing this?
  - What is the culture?

C) Apply: Ask, How does this apply to me, or to others?
  - Ask, "So what?" What does it mean to you?
  - What is he trying to move you to?

Third:

To find the main idea one must answer, "What is the author of the passage talking about?" and "What is he saying about what he is talking about?"

Author: _____ Time: _____

What is going on?

_____
_____
_____
_____
_____
_____
_____

Key Words:

_____

_____

_____

_____

_____

_____

Deal with the Text Objectively — Look at it objectively —
Let it speak for itself

Fourth: Read the Word with a Purpose — *Ask the following:*

<u>Who</u> wrote it? Who said it? Who are the major characters? Who are the people mentioned? To whom is the author speaking? About whom is the author speaking?

<u>What</u> are the main events? What are the major ideas? What are the major teachings? What are these people like? What does the author talk about most? What is the author's purpose in saying that?

<u>When</u> was it written? When did this event take place? When will it happen? When did he say it? When did he do it?

<u>Where</u> was this done? Where was this said? Where will it happen?

<u>Why</u> was there a need for this to be written? Why was this mentioned? Why was so much or so little space devoted to this particular event or teaching? Why was this reference mentioned? Why should they do such and such?

<u>How</u> is it done? How did it happen? How is this truth illustrated?

- Identifying information about the author and recipients:
    - o Who are they?
    - o What are their circumstances?
    - o What are their concerns?

- Examining the immediate context:
    - o Read the passages preceding and following the text
    - o Identify the key words or phrases
    - o Identify lists
    - o Note comparisons, contrasts, and conclusions
    - o Note time expressions
    - o Identify instructions or commands
    - o Outline or structure the text

o Identify why the author is writing (What is the author's purpose?)

o Identify the main theme of the book or passage

Interpretation

Interpretation answers the question: "What does this passage of scripture mean?" The basis for accurate interpretation is always careful observation. This is the process of discovering what the passage of scripture means. As you observe Scripture, the meaning will become apparent. One effective way to discover the meaning of a passage is by examining key words and consulting related cross-references.

By using a dictionary, a concordance, and other tools, you will gain a greater understanding of the author's intent and the message of the passage.

Word Studies — Examine the meaning of the word.

Identify the people: Read through the scripture(s) and mark in a distinctive way every person. Look for facts, names, gender, etc. (you can do this by highlights, circling the name (s), underline, etc.)

For Example:

2 Chronicles 7:14 " if my people, who are called by my name, will humble themselves and pray and seek my face and turn from their wicked ways, ***then*** *will I hear from heaven and will forgive their sin and will heal their land.*"

Simple word studies can be performed by consulting an English dictionary to clarify terms.

More advanced word studies can be performed by consulting an exhaustive concordance (for example, *Strong's Exhaustive Concordance of the Bible*). The concordance will provide the English transliteration of the original Greek or Hebrew word, the definition, and an exhaustive listing of each use of the word in the Bible.

Finally, an expository dictionary (for example, *Vine's Complete Expository Dictionary*) may be consulted for a more complete definition.

Cross-References—Consult other biblical passages where the word or concept occurs.

Finally we have; Application.

Application answers the question: "How does the meaning of this passage of scripture apply to me?" This is usually the first thing we want to know. Application takes place as you are confronted with the truth and decide to respond in obedience to that truth.

Ask yourself if the passage has one of these:

- A command to be obeyed
- A principle to be applied
- A warning to be heeded
- An illustration to be considered
- A consequence to be avoided

Tools that enhance application include these:

- Prayerful evaluation of the text
- Identification of specific principles, commands, instructions, or illustrations
- Memorization of verses (Psalm 119:11)

<u>KEY</u>— Accurate **interpretation** and correct **application** reset on the accuracy of your **observations**.

YOUR STORY

EXPOSING THE LIES AND LIVING THE TRUTH

_____

_____
_____
_____
_____
_____
_____
_____
_____
_____
_____
_____
_____
_____
_____
_____
_____

_____

_____

_____

_____

_____

_____

_____

_____

_____

_____

_____

_____

_____

_____

_____

_____

_____

_____

_____

_____

_____

_____

_____

_____

_____

_____

Your Story

REFERENCES

1. Joyce Meyer, *Battlefield of the Mind* (Hachette Book Group, Faith Words, 1995).
2. David Platt, *Radical*, (Multnomah Books, 2010).
3. Lisa Graham McMinn, *Growing Strong Daughters* (Baker Books, 2000, 2007, 2008).
4. Eugene Peterson, *The Message (NavPress Publishing Group, 1993, 1994, 1995, 1996, 2000, 2001, 2002).*
5. Valerie Bass, LISW-S.
6. Trina Pockett, inspirational speaker and writer – www.TrinaPockett.com

About the Author

Gail E. Dudley

"...bringing you closer to Christ."

With a commitment to delivering messages that are both scriptural and applicable to real life situations, Gail E. Dudley shares the words that are spoken into her heart by the Holy Spirit and delivers those messages to the listener's ear.

One of her most rewarding experiences was participating as a conference speaker in Bulawayo, Zimbabwe, Africa for The Women Unlimited of Word of Life International Annual Conference. Gail serves as a speaker and author with a passion to provide guidance to God's people as they navigate through their spiritual journey.

Currently Gail serves as a pastor at The Church at North Pointe, providing guidance, teaching discipleship studies, and overseeing multiple outreach efforts. She is also the Vice President of Diversity for Stonecroft Ministries, and works actively with the Mission America Coalition.

Gail is the wife of Reverend Dr. Kevin Dudley, senior pastor of The Church at North Pointe (Columbus, Ohio) and the loving mother of Alexander and Dominiq. Gail connects with people where they are in their journey and, upon hearing her speak, it is evident that Gail walks closely with the Lord, spends time daily in the Word and seeks always to be ready to share God's truth for transforming lives.

Booking Information

If you would like to schedule, Gail to speak at your retreat, your book club, or to do a book signing or a reading, please contact, Gail at:

<u>www.GailDudley.com</u>
<u>GED@MIMToday.org</u>
<u>614-441-8178</u>

We would love to hear from you. Send us your testimony and or prayer request.

To order additional books please go to Gail's website to order.

OTHER BOOKS BY GAIL

Ready to Change My Name ~
A Spiritual Journey from Fear to Faith

Ready to Pray ~
A Spiritual Journey of Praise and Worship

Ready to Pray (Workbook)

Ready to Pray (30 Minute Prayer CD)

Transparent Moments of Gail Dudley

ORDER ADDITIONAL COPIES TODAY

Gail E. Dudley
5550 Cleveland Avenue
Columbus, Ohio 43231-4049

Name: _____

Address: _____

City: _____ State: _____ Zip: _____

E-mail: _____

Would you like to join our mailing list? ❑ Yes ❑ No thank you.

Telephone: (___) _____ - _____

Ready to Change My Name	qty: _____	($15.00 each + $2.50 S & H)
Ready to Pray (the Book)	qty: _____	($15.00 each + $2.50 S & H)
Ready to Pray (215 page Workbook)	qty: _____	($24.95 each + $3.50 S & H)
Ready to Pray (30 Minute Prayer CD)	qty: _____	($7.00 each + $2.50 S & H)
Who Told You That?	qty: _____	($17.50 each + $3.00 S & H)
Transparent Moments	qty: _____	($7.00 each + $3.00 S & H)

Book Total: $ _____ S & H Total: _____ = Grand Total $_____

Number of books being shipped: _____

Please make checks payable to:
Gail E. Dudley

Send payment to:
5550 Cleveland Avenue, Columbus, Ohio 43231-4049

Please allow two (2) weeks for shipping

CPSIA information can be obtained
at www.ICGtesting.com
Printed in the USA
FFOW02n0437211017
41337FF